Voices of the 9/11 Pentagon
Recovery Effort

ALSO BY MARK JOSEPH MONGILUTZ

Solemn Duty in the Old Guard: From Arlington National Cemetery to the Pentagon on 9/11 in America's Oldest Regiment (2018)

Voices of the 9/11 Pentagon Recovery Effort

Essays from the U.S. Army's Old Guard

Edited by MARK JOSEPH MONGILUTZ

McFarland & Company, Inc., Publishers
Jefferson, North Carolina

LIBRARY OF CONGRESS CATALOGUING-IN-PUBLICATION DATA

Names: Mongilutz, Mark Joseph, editor.
Title: Voices of the 9/11 Pentagon recovery effort : essays from the U.S. Army's Old Guard / edited by Mark Joseph Mongilutz.
Other titles: Essays from the U.S. Army's Old Guard
Description: Jefferson, North Carolina : McFarland & Company, Inc., Publishers, 2020 | Includes index.
Identifiers: LCCN 2020020178 | ISBN 9781476680439 (paperback : acid free paper ∞) ISBN 9781476639475 (ebook)
Subjects: LCSH: United States. Army. Infantry Regiment, 3rd—History—21st century. | September 11 Terrorist Attacks, 2001. | Pentagon (Va.)—History—21st century. | Operation Noble Eagle, 2001—History.
Classification: LCC UA29 3d .V65 2020 | DDC 975.5/295044—dc23
LC record available at https://lccn.loc.gov/2020020178

BRITISH LIBRARY CATALOGUING DATA ARE AVAILABLE

ISBN 978-1-4766-8043-9 (paperback)
ISBN 978-1-4766-3947-5 (ebook)

© 2020 Mark Joseph Mongilutz. All rights reserved

No part of this book may be reproduced or transmitted in any form or by any means, electronic or mechanical, including photocopying or recording, or by any information storage and retrieval system, without permission in writing from the publisher.

On the cover: The Pentagon the evening after terrorists crashed American Airlines Flight 77 into the building on September 11, 2001 (Everett Historical, Shutterstock); Personnel sifting through debris inside the Pentagon following the attack on September 11, 2001, Arlington Virginia (FBI: The Vault).

Printed in the United States of America

McFarland & Company, Inc., Publishers
  Box 611, Jefferson, North Carolina 28640
  www.mcfarlandpub.com

Editor's Note

The work of editing a manuscript is at turns taxing and rewarding. It is a process requiring equal parts literary sensitivity, artistic instinct, and grammatical knowledge. And let's not leave out patience. One needs a good deal of that to visit and re-visit the same bodies of material as often as the process demands.

Editing the words of soldiers and veterans alongside whom I served so many years past was nothing short of an honor. It was also amusing at times. I was very often able to hear the *precise* inflection of a given contributor's authentic speaking voice; ensuring their written words wholly maintained possession of that authenticity was my guiding priority. To that end, I was careful to avoid reworking certain passages to my own liking if doing so would in any way disfigure a given contributor's communication style.

These essays adhere to convention on the whole but read in large measure as they were submitted. Minor corrections were expected by all who contributed, and I have done my part in that regard. Otherwise, the words you'll read are the words they wrote.

Table of Contents

Editor's Note — v

Preface — 1

Introduction
    MARK JOSEPH MONGILUTZ — 3

Private Memory
    ADAM BEHRENS — 7

Inside the 9/11 Pentagon Attack
    CHRISTOPHER M. BRADLEY — 17

Operation Noble Eagle
    DENNIS BRADY — 25

A Moment in Time
    LARRY CARTER II — 39

As I Saw Things
    MARSHALL R. CODD — 48

A Recent Richard's Recollection of His Time Recovering
    the Pentagon
    ERIC EBNER — 59

9/11 Revisited
    MATT GENKINGER — 66

A Witness to Bravery
    ANDY GRAFF — 75

Nights in White Coveralls
    JONATHAN HOFFMAN — 84

viii   Table of Contents

My Old Guard Fines E. Kiper II	98
The Impact of 9/11, Then and Now William Arthur Roum	109
We Laughed Brett (Thurman) SanPietro	117
America on Fire: A Grunt's Perspective Robert Earl Williams	126
For the Old Guard Soldiers Unsung and Unspoken Mark Joseph Mongilutz	144
Farewell: An Epilogue Mark Joseph Mongilutz	147
Glossary of Commonly Used Terms and Acronyms	149
About the Contributors	151
Index	153

Preface

I am unworthy of the honor and goodness which jointly circulate in and around this literary undertaking. That much is only true.

Collecting, editing, and sequencing the reflections, memories, and stories of so many good and extraordinary men has amounted to a relentless exercise in humility, one whose attendant labors have necessitated my coming to intimately know the wounded face of my foremost shortcomings ... its every line, scar, and blemish.

But the work needs to be done. It does.

It does.

Though seemingly having befallen our nation an abbreviated eon past, the events of September 11, 2001, seem almost immediately current when their images find purchase upon our eyes, when the trauma they yielded resurfaces from the soil of suppressed memory, when the toll they exacted assumes personal, rather than monumental, form.

For reasons both understandable and inevitable, the colloquially termed "9/11 attacks" are most symbolically linked to the World Trade Center and, by extension, to New York City itself. The Pentagon's destruction was chronicled to a lesser degree via televisual broadcast than were the streets surrounding the World Trade Center, and the brutal collision it absorbed was not (to my knowledge) captured via civilian camcorder.

Again, for reasons as understandable as they are inevitable, the Pentagon tends to exist somewhat on the periphery of our nation's collective 9/11 memory. With several exceptions—the men and women, military and civilian both, who took part to one degree or another in the recovery effort, in extinguishing the hostile fires, in tending to the wounded, in supporting the first responders and the tireless laborers. And to this should very much be added those servicemembers and government workers who were present in the Pentagon when it was struck, but whose lives were spared by virtue of not occupying, in that fatal moment, the area of impact.

The stories herein collectively capture a specific chapter of the Pentagon recovery effort—the one enacted by soldiers of the 3rd United States Infantry Regiment (the Old Guard), the Army's oldest infantry unit still operating in an active duty capacity.

I closely chronicled my individual account of the Pentagon Recovery Effort in my memoir *Solemn Duty in the Old Guard* and did so with the aim of conveying elements both emotional and narratively factual for the reader's benefit. And while I would not change so much as a syllable of my writings therein, they capture the thoughts of but a single soldier—one man, one limited perspective, one crop of memories.

But the hunger for a more complete picture of the recovery process far exceeds the yield of a single crop's finite harvest.

So it is that I have enlisted the hearts and recollections of several of my Old Guard brothers, some of whom I served immediately alongside during the effort, some of whom I saw infrequently if at all until our part in the process had come to an end. The collection serves as a literary dais from which these regimental veterans will impart upon you what they remember, relate to you what they have learned, and render themselves emotionally unarmored throughout.

They will do so functionally in succession, but spiritually in unison. Theirs are voices harmonized in service to a tale worth immortalizing, to pain worth acknowledging, to camaraderie worth celebrating, to sacrifice worth honoring, to truth worth embalming, to wisdom worth echoing, to innocence worth resuscitating, to a national unity worth reclaiming.

These are the voices of my brothers. Hear them, as I have, and come away better for it … as I have.

Introduction

Mark Joseph Mongilutz

Was any of it real? *Any* of it?

The answer, of course, is yes. It was much too real. It just wasn't what we had expected. Not one among us. How could we? How could anyone?

Like so many of those with whom I served in the Old Guard, I had joined the Army during the tail-end of Bill Clinton's presidency. And while the 1990s were not necessarily a halcyon period for all human beings, they were certainly such a period for many middle-class Americans. Prosperity and happiness were effectively our republic's co-consuls throughout the final years of the 20th century, the occasional small-scale crisis and aberrational act of domestic terrorism notwithstanding.

Indeed, we were troubled by a few problems of our own making, but, in the aggregate, things were stable, peaceable, good. Economic inequality was certainly manifest, but the civil strife that now stems from it was far less hostile than is now the case. Social fissures were extant, but we had not yet seen fit to once again trace battle lines atop them.

All was not perfect, but most was largely well. Largely.

So it was in the Old Guard, at least from what I gathered between Thanksgiving of 2000 and September 10 of 2001.

As I said: Most was largely well.

Largely.

There was a sense that, though we were serving in uniform, our duty was that of peacetime warriors. If ever there was a more pronounced example of professional incongruity, I've yet to encounter it.

We had been trained to kill and to endure hardship, but only a highly diluted form of the latter was on offer at the Old Guard. Killing was off the menu and the diluted hardship, such as it was, stemmed solely from the profession's physical demands, as well as from the mental burden of tending to the dead on so regular a basis.

Intensive uniform maintenance and strict physical training expectations are demanding, to be sure, but Old Guard soldiers tend to adapt fairly quickly. It's novel at first, familiar within a month, and perfectly manageable by the time you've consumed your fiftieth chow hall breakfast.

From that point forth, it's a matter of tracking your ceremonies and funerals, keeping fit, enjoying your time away from it all when possible, and making/revising your post–Old Guard plans. It is, in short, a job. You figure out where you fit into the larger scheme, stay more or less in line, take bi-annual leave, maybe transfer to a specialty platoon if you're so inclined, and perhaps make E-5/Sergeant prior to returning your dress blues and placing ceremonial duty behind you.

That's effectively how things had worked for some time prior to my arrival in the autumn of 2000 and how they worked for the better part of a year thereafter. That would have been a fine way to serve out my enlistment and was how so many Old Guardsmen before me had served out their own.

But the juggernaut of human history, wielding a hammer fist of tragedy, would render the simplicity of that Old Guard model untenable for a time.

The Pentagon was hit. The Old Guard was nearby. The story changed mid-chapter. Suddenly, tallying Arlington National Cemetery (ANC) missions, pressing uniforms, and rendering our precision movements still more precise all found themselves relegated to a lower tier within the regiment's collective priority list. What became clear was that our primary mission would be subjected to change due to exigent circumstances. And what was 9/11 if not exigency defined?

We saw many of the the same things.

We all internalized them distinctively.

I remember things others do not; others remember things I almost certainly did not see or would subsequently suppress. The tragedy was apparent to all of us, but the coping response developed in ways quite unique to each soldier's respective mind. Christopher M. Bradley, my team leader at the time, recalls an exchange that transpired between us within the ruins of the Pentagon. I don't recall it all. But, then, there are gaps. Some things we should all remember are instead remembered by a few. Some things are clear at times and opaque at others. It's a frustrating limitation with which to grapple; still, here we are, grappling.

We had all reported to the Old Guard with the understanding that we would deal with the dead in a sterile, polished, orderly capacity. The regiment's part in the Pentagon Recovery Effort necessitated our confronting death in its most appalling and scarring form. As several of my brothers have observed, it was somehow fitting in a horrid sort of way. You see, Old Guard service forces the living and the dead into an enduring union of sorts. While we were accustomed to that union manifesting on our own ceremonial terms, the terrorist attacks of September 11, 2001, mandated our doing so in ways obscene, grotesque, and regrettably necessary.

I occasionally afford myself the psychological indulgence of an overly favorable assessment of my confrontation with that obscenity, grotesqueness, and necessity. Which is to say, I imagine my work there to have been an exercise in nobility, a worthy expression of military duty, of service to country, to humanity, to something higher than myself.

But this indulgence tends to wilt swiftly when subjected to the sunlight of objective scrutiny. I did what was asked of me. I did not work as hard as did others, nor was I as invested psychologically as were so many others. Some were burdened by great pain in the aftermath, some were not; some could not bring themselves to see our work there as anything other than a few weeks of physically taxing labor.

Still, the notion of the Recovery Effort having been an inherently noble cause is a notion I have worked actively to preserve and justify. Many of this work's contributors have ostensibly done the same.

You will find the essays herein relate stories as similar in the feelings they channel as they are distinctive in the details they emphasize. Some traffic in powerful emotion while others deliver close accountings of our daily work. Take from it what you will but give to it your close attention. My brothers deserve that much.

With two exceptions, the essays to come are theirs.

Private Memory

Adam Behrens

My life before the Army and the Old Guard was that of a typical high school student. I grew up in Northern Michigan's Upper Peninsula in the city of Marquette. Aside from attending class, I enjoyed hiking, shooting, fishing, four-wheeling down old dirt roads, and just about any outdoor activity. I was extremely competitive but decided not to participate in normal high school sports, instead focusing that competitiveness on my close group of friends; we all tried to beat each other in activities such as shooting, racing, video games, and any other random high school extracurricular undertakings.

Life in the Upper Peninsula, in retrospect, was much different than that of kids growing up in highly populated areas. My pastimes reflected the outdoors and the pace of life was much slower. I found myself after high school with a job working as a prep cook in one of the nicest restaurants downtown and living in a small studio apartment with a close friend. It was after about six months of surviving on my own that I started to become aware of my future and what little the small town had to offer me for the rest of my life. I started to become depressed as I looked around to see what other careers I could pursue and realized there was not much that would satisfy my sense of competition and need for adventure. I recall having heard a quote early in life, though I cannot recall just when it became instilled in my brain. It was something along the lines of "taking the path less traveled," but manifested itself in my head as "taking the hardest possible path life presents you."

It was late one night after a party with friends that I found myself stumbling home through the backstreets of town with too much beer and liquor in my underage system. I was angry that I had to work in the morning (hungover) and contemplated calling in sick to work. I randomly took a left down a quiet neighborhood street to cut across Main Street to my side of town and took a rest on the Post Office steps. While sitting there, I noticed a sign in the window advertising enlistment in the Armed Services. I then realized the military recruitment offices shared a building with the Post Office.

I had never contemplated joining the military, but the next day, while hungover at work, I could not stop thinking about what my life would be like at sea with the Navy or in some camp with the Marine Corps. I daydreamed about movies I remembered seeing, video games I've played, and placed myself in different roles. I decided to swing by the recruitment offices after work to get some flyers and information.

Upon entering the Post Office, I found my way to the lower level where the recruitment offices were located. Each branch of service had their own office; I was immediately intimidated by the sight of the various men in uniform. I quickly grabbed some information in the small lobby and left before anyone noticed I was there.

That evening, I decided to drive home and talk to my parents who were both surprised and worried about my newfound interest. My mother didn't like the idea, but my father told me to call some of my family members who had served and family friends who could give me better advice. Over the week, both my parents and I spoke with various family and friends, and I became more and more excited with the challenge of joining the military. Most of friends were supportive, however, a few told me I was crazy. Based on my limited research, I decided I wanted to join the Army, as most of my relatives served in the Army and I was told they had the most opportunities.

The following week, I worked up the courage to meet the Army recruiter. He was a very laidback gentleman in a camouflage uniform which I would later know as the Battle Dress Uniform (BDUs). He spoke to me about everything the Army had to offer, including money toward college, known as the GI Bill. This information helped solidify my decision, as I always wanted to attend college but didn't know how I could afford it or what degree to pursue. The recruiter told me there was no immediate pressure and encouraged me to take an exam to determine what jobs I could apply for and told me to start working out. He informed me that if I passed a basic Army Physical Fitness Test (APFT), I would go in at a higher rank.

Upon leaving the recruiter's office, my mind was made up—I was going to join the Army! That same day I quit my job and told my roommate I was moving out. I soon moved back in with my parents and began a workout regimen that included running and a ton of pushups, sit-ups and pull-ups. Over the next couple of months, I passed my exam and the APFT. The recruiter told me I scored extremely high on my exam and I could apply for any job within the Army. He encouraged me to join military intelligence. As smart as I was, military intelligence was just not sexy to my imagination; nope, I wanted to join the Infantry and maybe become a Ranger or a member of the

Special Forces. Images of Rambo and the Predator were in my mind, and all I wanted to do was blow shit up and shoot guns!

The following months brought me to Milwaukee for my physical examination, then to Fort Benning, GA, for Infantry training. I had an Army Ranger contract with Airborne School, as well. However, as fate had it, my height, weight, and exam score met the requirements for the Old Guard. I was pulled into the Old Guard recruitment office in the beginning stages of Basic Training, where the recruiter told me how much more elite the Old Guard was instead of being a "bullet-catching Ranger." The recruiter told me only the best and brightest could be a part of the Old Guard. Every infantry member could become a Ranger in the future, but few were afforded the opportunity of serving in the Old Guard within their career. He further told me he could work it out that I still attended Airborne School and that I better agree soon, as there were only so many slots available. This sounded great to me and I eagerly said yes!

Arrival to Fort Myer after Basic Training and Airborne School was exciting, to say the least. This was my first time in Washington, D.C., and really my first time living in a major metropolitan area. Flying into Reagan National Airport, I had my face glued to the window as I looked below at the National Mall. I could not wait to get downtown and see all the history and the museums. Upon arrival to my unit, I was assigned to the marching platoon whose duty it was to stand in formation during funerals. I was given a room and told I would soon be attending training. My only duty at this point was to arrive at morning formation for physical training and complete in-processing. Everyone called me a "New DICK" (Dedicated Infantry Combat Killer), and I made it my goal to keep my head low and stay out of sight and mind until I was past this introductory phase. Everyone liked to pick on the new guys.

After a few months, I had learned how to dress and take care of my uniforms, completed the Regimental Orientation Program (ROP) training that taught me how to march, and started working with my platoon full time. I had time to explore Washington, D.C., on the weekends during this time and had made a few close friends who were also new. One of my fondest early memories was running into Washington, D.C., and along the Mall during physical training early in the morning.

As I learned more about the Old Guard, I became aware of "special duties" available to soldiers. To name a few, you could join the Drill Team, which performed rifle acrobatics in front of audiences, the Caisson Platoon, which worked with the horses to transfer the departed within Arlington National Cemetery, the Tomb Guards, who guard the Tomb of the Unknown Soldier, and Pentagon tour guide, which afforded soldiers the opportunity to work inside the Pentagon and learn everything about it. Of all the special duties, I was determined to work at the Pentagon, which I achieved later in my service.

September 11, 2001

On the fateful day of September 11, 2001, I had a dental appointment in the morning. I was in a good mood, since this meant missing the morning's physical training. It was nice to have a break every so often. The dental office was located on post a couple blocks away from the Pentagon. While I was in the waiting room, I noticed a television was on without volume and it was showing a plane had crashed into a skyscraper in New York. At that moment my name was called, and I headed back and climbed into the dental chair. The hygienist came into the room and made small talk and asked if I saw the freak accident in New York. I acknowledged that I saw the accident and we both were bewildered at how such a horrific accident could happen. The real situation still being unknown to us, she proceeded to clean my teeth and make casual talk. About halfway through the cleaning, we heard a loud explosion that reminded me of a large truck backfiring. We were both startled at the noise, but assumed it was nothing of importance. Little did we know the sound was American Airlines Flight 77 striking the Pentagon.

After my cleaning, I reported back to work. As I walked into the foyer of my company, known as the dayroom, about a dozen of my fellow soldiers were crowded around the television. I didn't think much of this and proceeded to ask someone nearby if they knew where my squad was. They looked at me and said they didn't know and asked if I knew what was happening. I shrugged, as I was still clueless, despite what I had already seen and heard. They told me we were under attack and an enemy had struck the Twin Towers and the Pentagon. A sergeant in the dayroom then told me my squad was training in another building and that I was to run over there and bring them back as soon as possible. I asked him if they knew which building and received a properly stupid stare and typical sergeant response of, "How the fuck should I know? Go, now!" I ran.

Adrenaline was pumping as I realized the backfiring truck I had heard at my appointment was the plane hitting the Pentagon, a million thoughts were racing through my brain. Were we going to war? Was someone trying to invade? Were bombs being dropped elsewhere? Why would anyone do this? I had to call my parents. I had to find my squad. I ran through an almost-abandoned building on base where my squad was supposed to be training. After a few floors I found them. Out of breath, I entered the room to find everyone staring at me. "Why the hell are you out of breath, Private?" asked my squad leader. I told them all we were under attack, that New York had

An image of the damaged Pentagon from afar; notice the helicopters patrolling immediately above (photograph by Photographer's Mate 2nd Class R. Deuce Rubio, USN).

been hit and also the Pentagon. At first, they thought I was joking, but the seriousness on my face said otherwise. I told them we had to get back to the company. We quickly left.

Back at the company, it was chaos. None of us knew the extent of the situation. All personnel were being mustered and rumors were flying among the rank and file. It appeared we were going to draw weapons and ammunition in preparation for the worst. My cell phone was not working, and it took me almost an hour to get a call through to my mother. I told her I was all right and that we were all at base preparing for the worst. She told me to be careful and to check in periodically with updates. I waited with everyone for further instructions and information. The act, we shortly knew, was from a foreign enemy and our first mission was to get to the Pentagon for recovery efforts.

The whole ordeal was a blur of sleeplessness and confusion from my perspective as a young soldier. I knew nothing but to follow orders and prepare for the unknown. Certain aspects of the recovery are burned into my brain, while many others escape my memory, most likely due to the lack of rest and maybe some sort of coping mechanism. The following is what I remember almost eighteen years later.

I remember the fighter jets flying overhead tearing across the D.C.

skyline. They were flying low and you could feel them in your chest as they flew overhead. Car alarms were going off due to their low altitude. Our company was forming up in the quad (which was an outdoor open space much like a courtyard behind and in-between the company building). Our Company Commander was speaking, as was our First Sergeant. Their instructions were falling on deaf ears, as my mind was elsewhere.

Before I knew it, I was climbing aboard a five-ton M939 personnel truck and driving down into Crystal City, which is next to the Pentagon. We were packed into the truck like sardines. People were everywhere, all walking away from the crash site. It was surreal seeing so many people in business attire walking all in the same direction away from the Pentagon. Police were everywhere directing traffic and pedestrians. We didn't go directly onsite; I believe we were supposed to secure some area nearby. We ended up across a highway from the Pentagon, there were various camera crews staged there. The site of the burning Pentagon was stark.

That same day, I believe, we entered Arlington National Cemetery directly across from the Pentagon and collected debris from the plane impact. I remember scanning the grounds for any material. I spoke to one soldier from a different Company who was performing a funeral during the time of the crash at that same general location. He was in a firing squad whose mission was to perform the twenty-one-gun salute during funeral proceedings. He said he was standing at attention in the cemetery and saw the plane directly hit the Pentagon. He saw the faces of people looking out the plane's windows as it went down. He said it felt like slow motion as he stood there, helpless, not understanding what he was seeing before him.

We completed many minor missions for a couple of days after the attack, but most of the time we waited in anticipation of performing some kind of duty. Once the fire departments contained the blaze of jet fuel and confirmed the general stability of the structure, we were tasked with entering the crash site to retrieve classified documents, plane parts, and casualties. Once again, we loaded up on the five-ton trucks and headed towards the crash site. This time, as we closely approached, everyone grew silent and nothing could describe the smell in the air.

Once on site, we erected tents, as we were going to be there for a while. A plurality of tents had been set up by the various departments already undergoing the cleanup and recovery effort. I remember all sorts of volunteers onsite giving out free food, massages, clothes, toiletries, blankets, etc. A vast majority of skills and needs all came together in that moment. At one point, I saw the American flag being draped over the side of the Pentagon by the fire department.

At this time, our company was split up into different groups to perform different missions. Only so many could enter the crash site safely and we would be taking shifts so we could work around the clock. Some of us entered the undamaged portion of the Pentagon and were in charge of testing air quality, I believe, but was I never tasked with this job. Another group from the company was to head to a large parking area to guard any and all plane parts recovered, once again I was never tasked with this duty so am unable to confirm the exact details of those missions. Our group's mission was entering the crash site and to start the cleanup.

The first time we entered the crash site, we were in our BDUs, basic camouflage attire, with leather gloves and our military helmets. We were carrying our E-Tool shovels and were outfitted with basic breathing masks like the ones one would use for painting and found at any home improvement store. Our squad leader also had some sort of chemical sensing device, within 30 feet of entering the device sounded off. One of my fellow squad members asked what it meant, our squad leader said that we shouldn't take off our masks and proceeded to turn off the machine.

Upon entering, it was like a maze of burnt debris and we immediately saw gruesome death in detail I won't describe. We dug through this death separating paper from people and both of these from the plane. Others were aiding the recovery effort inside to include the FBI, from what I recall. The work was tiring, several of us removed our masks and took breaks within an inner ring of the Pentagon, but not immediately within the crash site; in hindsight, this was probably not a good idea. The notion of a black box was mentioned. At the time, I did not know the significance of this item in relation to the plane. We continued to work, sifting through the debris and wading through areas of varying depth water and jet fuel for an unknown time period until we were relieved by the next squad.

Upon exiting the crash site, we were directed to cleaning tents as we were all covered in unknown contaminants. We were instructed to strip down naked and were hosed off and scrubbed down with large soft-bristled brushes full of soap. For some unknown reason, this did not alarm me, as I was merely doing my job and didn't think anything of it. However, within the next few days we were fully outfitted in double-layered hazardous material (hazmat) suits with better breathing apparatuses and filters. The cleaning tent routine continued each time we left the site.

I cannot accurately tell how many days we took turns entering and exiting the site. I guess we did this for about a week. We worked inside, we exited and were decontaminated, we slept on-site in tents, and we waited. Some shifts were in the dead of night. Entering the crash site and dealing with the horrific scene at night was somehow different than in the day. During this time, I also fractured my wrist during cleanup. I did not know it was broken at the time but saw a PA, who provided Motrin, and I got back to work. Maybe it was the surreal fog due to the intensity of the situation mixed with a lack of sleep. Maybe it was a human coping mechanism. Whatever it was, it just didn't seem real. Every time I found something, I called to the appropriate authorities for assistance. Plane parts and paper went with who I believe were FBI, who took it off somewhere. The rest of what I found went into black bags and was taken for identification/testing purposes.

A weird phenomenon I came to realize years later, when pondering the situation, was the human reaction to such a tragic event by those who must physically deal with carnage is sometimes laughter. Not by or for everyone involved, as some remained solemn in their duties; however, a handful of us filled the silent time with jokes and mirth. Some may feel disdain at the very idea of laughing during such a situation, and often I have thought back and wondered if we were behaving inappropriately or were somehow disrespectful to the dead. I realize now that there is no behavior that is inappropriate in the face of such a task. Anyone who judges from the outside has never experienced anything close to what we experienced in there. Further, everyone's reaction to death in such a raw state is different. Humor allowed some to carry on.

In one instance, I was done being scrubbed down and exited the tent naked with a couple of small towels to dry off with. Some of the guys were goofing around and slapping each other with towels. Across the way we heard laughing and noticed a handful of young FBI girls watching us. Of course, this only spurred us on to show off and mess around even more. Later that day, while I was visiting the food tents, I ran across one of those young FBI girls and had a brief and awkward conversation, the specifics of which are lost to me now. We randomly met a couple months later and started dating that year; we are happily married today with two kids. Each year we try to come back to the Pentagon for the 9/11 Remembrance Ceremony outside of the Pentagon to pay our respects to those who lost their lives and to keep the memory of the event alive.

After our main recovery effort, we completed an after-action report (AAR). We indicated that we were possibly exposed to hazardous chemicals per instruction from our squad leader. In hindsight, our team leader understood the possibility that we may have been indeed placed in harm's way, and he did the right thing by telling us to take the AAR seriously, and to fill it out accurately. In the moment, we were all proud of our service and still are proud today; but the thought still lingers as to what made that chemical sensor go off and if we were exposed to any really harmful chemicals that may one day compromise the well-being of one, some, or all of us.

We were further offered psychological aid in the chance we were struggling with any part of what we were exposed to. This offer was laughed off by the majority of those around me, and by me. At the time, we were all too hardcore and seeking any help in this manner would be considered weak. I sure didn't want to approach my superiors and tell them what I saw had a profound effect on me. The truth is that we all experienced different things during the recovery effort, and each person dealt with what they saw differently. Personally, I pulled things from the rubble that I wish I never saw nor had to physically deal with. In the moment, I simply carried on, placed what I found in a black bag and pretended it didn't faze me. Of course, anyone who tells you a serious experience does not change or alter them in some way is either in denial or not fully in touch with their inner emotions and thoughts. I would not change anything I did in my duty, nor do I have any regrets, but this experience did have a profound effect on me and is a part of what shaped me into the person I am today.

One thing I learned about myself after seeing and touching death is that I didn't want anything to do with it from that point forward. I was not an overly religious individual but my belief in God told me that the path going forward was one of love and had nothing to do with violence and loss. I struggled with this notion inside my head, I had wanted to further my military career and become a Ranger or join the Special Forces. I had an instilled pride and competitive nature that viewed this very feeling as weakness of character. I did not want to be a quitter, I wanted to better my military prowess. I am not a person who lives in fear, or for that matter, fears their own death. In fact, I welcome the inevitable fact. But I concluded that my path going forward was not with the military, did not include following the orders of others, and did not have anything to do with dealing with death anymore. In hindsight, the military path was in a way too easy, too comfortable. Leaving pulled me out of an unknown comfort zone which I had become accustomed to.

Before leaving military service, I was proud to attain a special assignment position working within the Pentagon as a tour guide. This was an early goal of mine and an even bigger goal after experiencing the 9/11 attacks. For one year, I learned everything I could about the building and its history. I met many generals, civilian leaders, people involved in the recovery, people who experienced the attack from within the building, and fellow servicemembers from various branches. Each branch was represented in the tour guide program and I gained friends I still have today. After 9/11, two memorials were built, one inside the Pentagon where the plane impacted the building and another outside the Pentagon more accessible to the public. During each tour, we visited the internal memorial and I spoke of my experiences during the recovery effort. I was honored to be a part of this program. It was the height of my enlistment experience.

I left the Army in 2005 and immediately sensed a loss of worth, as I was a civilian. Civilian life was different and unstructured and, at first, I saw it as less meaningful. I considered reenlisting and reached out to different enlistment branches and was told no one needed infantry-skilled veterans except for the Army. I considered going back into the infantry but reminded myself I would be taking the familiar path and instead found new ways to challenge myself. I went to college and achieved a degree in civil/mechanical engineering with a focus on environmental engineering. I also got married to Ashley (whom I mentioned earlier meeting at the Pentagon crash site during the 9/11 cleanup) and had two children. I continued working for the government in the Army Corps of Engineers, Department of Transportation, Federal Highway Administration, and the Patent and Trademark Office. Working and growing a family was, and still is, my greatest achievement in life. It was a harder challenge than I expected and made me change as a person in ways which I found to be a greater test to myself than anything else that came before.

Looking back at the military and watching close friends still serving, I now know I made the right choices for myself and my family. Military combat service comprises a plethora of experiences that I know would have shaped me in a completely different manner. My close friends who have chosen to make a career of military service, and all others who do so, have my respect and admiration. Military service comes with a great sacrifice to self and family. Because of my experiences, my wife and I make it a point to raise our children with knowledge of and respect for our police and military. We choose to donate time and money to various veteran services, mainly those that focus on post-traumatic stress and physical impairment; and we maintain close and personal relationships with friends who are still in and are about to retire.

In closing, when I reflect on my military experiences, and those surrounding 9/11, I am proud of my time served and proud of those who decide to serve. I will continue to give where I can and am proud to be an American. The country came together over those terrible events in a way only America can. We should all be grateful to live in the greatest country and among the greatest people on the face of the earth.

Inside the 9/11 Pentagon Attack

Christopher M. Bradley

I've told a hundred different versions of this story, all catered to the audience in front of me. It's the same story with details added or left out to protect the audience. Out of respect for my brothers, I'll tell it straight with nothing left out.

Where to begin? I guess I joined the military for the same patriotic reasons most people do, but the manner in which I enlisted is a story more worth telling. I was born in New Jersey, took a brief two-year stop in Florida, and was raised in North Carolina. "The Tarheel State" as President George W. Bush once referred to it during a five-second conversation I had with him during my service in the Old Guard. I'm getting ahead of myself.

I grew up in North Carolina in a blended family as the oldest of five siblings and fought everyone who challenged me. My yearbooks are filled with comments that say as much. I wasn't a bad kid, and there was potential; with the help of some positive role models I was able to complete high school without a criminal record. When I graduated, my plan was to wrestle for the Marine Corps and work as a Military Police Officer, but fate showed me how brittle the plans of teenagers can be.

In the weeks before I took my oath, I was injured in a way that disbarred me from service. I was devastated. My recruiter knew about the injury and he terminated my packet. I'm intentionally being vague because what I'm going to say next has caused me shame most of my life, and I pride myself on being honest and trustworthy. A few weeks later while I was still recovering at home, a female Army recruiter showed up at my parents' house showering me with compliments about my high ASVAB (Armed Services Vocational Aptitude Battery) score and physique. She told me the only job I couldn't enlist for was that of Astronaut, and that's only because they weren't currently hiring.

(Side note: I would totally have signed up for Space Force but after watching the badass Infantry video, there's no way I was signing up for anything else.)

My Marine Corps physical was still valid, so I joined the Army while no one was looking and a few days later I found myself in Fort Benning at the fabled 2/58 "House of Pain." During my Infantry training, I must have impressed my sadistic platoon cadre, because I was promoted to team leader for two-thirds of basic training. I took great pride in taking the worst situations in stride. During that time I also attended an "invite only" meeting to speak with the 3rd U.S. Infantry "the Old Guard" recruiters who again showed me a video that I could not resist. I abandoned my promised Airborne Ranger contract for the opportunity to defend our nation's capital. After a quick phone call to my mother for approval, the deal was done.

The only advice my Drill Sergeant gave me about the Old Guard was this: "In the first five minutes, someone will decide whether you're standing on the White House lawn or shoveling horseshit for the next four years." I later ran into that same Drill Sergeant (he'd been promoted to E-8/1st Sergeant) at Air Assault School a few years later. He walked up to me in formation, sniffed me, smiled, told me I didn't smell like horseshit, and walked away smiling. Moving forward, the Old Guard was, if nothing else, a machine. Soldiers showed up as chewed bubblegum and learned how to do something. They could be doing anything from shoveling shit to throwing rifles twenty feet in the air. I learned how to carry caskets and fold flags, a task I'm sure I performed thousands of times during missions and thousands more practicing. I learned from the seasoned soldiers before me and passed that knowledge on to the newer soldiers as they arrived. There was a healthy competition within my company, Bravo Company, whose motto was "Battlehard," and the regiment's other companies. We trained to fight, we performed thousands of hours of ceremonies, we did stupid things in our off time, and we grew close. But that 60-hour work week isn't what this retelling is about so let's move on.

September 11, 2001, started off as a normal day. There was work to be done inside the beehive of Bravo Company. I was in my Class A uniform when the dayroom staff shouted into the hallway that some "dumb fucker" flew a plane into a World Trade Center tower. As I made my way into the dayroom to watch the footage another plane followed suit. We were under attack. At this point in my military career, I'd been promoted to Sergeant. I was acting team leader over a gaggle of "new dicks" who had been recently transformed from pathetic to acceptable Old Guard soldiers. Yes, I was hard on them. We had a hard job with no room for mistakes and I'd spent the better part of the summer trying to turn these nineteen- and twenty-year-old kids into "Battlehard" soldiers. Aside from our ceremonial duties, we also trained as Infantry soldiers at Fort AP Hill and rarely at Fort Polk, Louisiana. When we were not training, the days consisted of busy work, exercise, and impromptu hand-to-hand combat. Within the walls of our company we created secret locations known as "The Octagon." We also had a reputation for ambushing other platoons, physically overpowering them, and placing a black dye "brand" on them. It didn't burn, but it did leave a mark. No one was safe, even Battlehard's Executive Officer (XO) suffered our wrath on a field exercise. All fun and games aside, nothing we'd trained for prepared us for 9/11 except that we were a family.

I was a part of a brief meeting. And by brief, I mean it was no longer than a minute. I remember being told we were going to the Capitol to assist Capitol Police with a possible "dirty bomb." I can remember thinking, "What in the hell could we do against a bomb?" By the time the Pentagon was struck we'd already changed into BDUs (Battle Dress Uniform) and boarded buses to be deployed into Washington, D.C. Information flowed like molasses on a cold Wisconsin morning. We knew nothing. Our chain of command knew as much as we did. I remember hearing sonic booms in the sky and wondering if it was the bomb I'd heard about minutes earlier. Spotting our own jets was a relief, but after seeing the destruction we witnessed as the buses exited Fort Myer and came into view of the Pentagon, that relief quickly faded away. I later found out from my wife that the impact at the Pentagon was forceful enough to shake our apartment at Tenza Terrace (base housing at Fort Myer, VA) less than a mile away. The hijacked commercial plane would have flown past our high-rise apartment to hit the Pentagon. The building shaking woke up my firstborn infant daughter in her crib. I still think about that event like I'm standing over her when it happens. My sweet innocent daughter Loren. This visual makes me angry and it's crossed my mind no fewer than a thousand times over the years. I'm sure it always will. It wakes up something inside of me that I've spent a lifetime trying to lull to sleep.

If my memory serves me correctly, we parked in the middle of the highway and made short work of a construction fence to enter the Pentagon property. This part of the property was littered with construction equipment, notably a crane. Even at 100 or so yards, the Pentagon was massive and majestic as it had always been … except for the collapsed portion facing us. The fireball and copious smoke pouring from its center was already visible for miles. Fire engines arrived and their operators pulled into the crash site and did what they could, shooting streams of water at the entrance. Ambulances tended to the walking wounded and crowds of people stood on the bridge behind us. We stood there with our proverbial "thumbs up our asses," having nothing to do. We were grunts awaiting grunt work. We'd been ambushed and training says to assault through the ambush. Assault who? There was no enemy, only destruction. That afternoon consisted mostly of building tents

A ground level Pentagon view closely depicting the extensive damage absorbed by the structure (photograph by PH2 Robert Houlihan, USN).

and asking questions that could never have been answered. I'm sure I had heartfelt conversations with my soldiers and friends but all of these years later all I can remember with certainty was my anger. In the words of country music artist Toby Keith, "A sucker punch." I agree with Keith: that's *exactly* what it was.

I had a casual conversation with a military engineer who explained we needed to tunnel inside to support the other parts of the building from collapsing. It was obvious from the outside that the structure suffered considerable damage and then started to collapse on itself. When the order finally came, we assumed our place in line and started working our way into a small opening beside the impact site. When we finally entered the building that afternoon, we did ant's work. A line of soldiers tunneling into the building moving one piece of rubble at a time.

Someone hands me something gnarled and broken and I hand it to the person behind me. The debris was passed from soldier to soldier until it exited the building and was sorted. Two piles: airplane and building. I was told before entering that someone from the airline company was already there to identify plane parts. We didn't find many obvious plane pieces at first, a small piece occasionally. The nose of the plane actually made it to the inner wall of the Pentagon. A third pile started later in the evening, the body bags.

Bodies and body parts were photographed as they were discovered. The remains were bagged and carried outside of the building by a separate team. The building was dark and water soaked my boots and pants. I can only speak for my own state of mind when I say that I was honored to be helping and terrified of what was going on around me. What was happening in the world? Was the attack continuing? Was a military force making its way towards our borders or had they already infiltrated? The smell was so strong and overpowered our expired protective mask filters. The physical toll nulled the racing mind and we worked for hours. If I had to describe it, maybe burned concrete could suffice, but it was more morbid than that because we knew death was present. We buried people in Arlington having never personally known them. Only their families were present, and it was our duty to show respect for the service of their loved one with as close to flawless-as-possible precision—this was our craft. This death was a different type of death, it was murder of our countrymen. It was an emotional time for all of us. I can remember a young soldier named Private Mongilutz on my team asking to exit the building because he felt sick. I yelled at him telling him to suck it up. We had a job to do and we needed to deal with the vulgar nature of the job. Years later I would apologize for treating him this way and ignoring his needs for the sake of the mission. He was a good kid, just soft around the edges. Something changed inside of me that evening and I can only assume it's the same for many of my brothers inside the bowels of the Pentagon that evening. When you watch a movie, you see death, mayhem, explosions, and carnage. We view these movies as entertainment. Since that day, I don't equate it as entertainment, it's a lesson. In layman's terms, it makes it all real, all possible and that way of thinking can destroy you if you don't keep it in check. The day made us all a little more "Battlehard" for better or worse. By the time we exited the building, the sun had been down for hours and speaking for myself, I was completely spent emotionally and physically.

During the night, the support services began to arrive. Outback, McDonald's, Red Cross, and the Southern Baptist Men were there feeding everyone at the crash site and offering clean socks and clothing. I was so proud of the Southern Baptist Men, because as a child I'd heard them being referred to in church during fundraisers. I asked questions about the condition of the world outside of our crash site and got some answers that put my mind to rest, somewhat. Four planes went down, no other attacks. An Islamic group I'd never heard of took credit. I was thankful my enemy had a name.

We then slept under the tents we'd put up earlier. By the time we entered the building hours later, the other infantry companies had finished clearing debris from the first floor. I assume they used some small frontend loaders to remove every piece of debris for examination. Whatever method they used, they did a tremendous job. The first floor was unrecognizable from the hours prior. It was during this trip into the Pentagon that I was able to walk all the way into the Pentagon's inner wall and see the courtyard and the breach caused by the plane. The remaining plane debris was being cut into smaller pieces and removed. The courtyard was a breath of fresh air. It was a peaceful green oasis in a world of destruction. That same day I took a small group of soldiers to the second floor to start removing furniture, filing cabinets, etc. The floor we were standing on seemed stable enough but the words of the engineer the day before were living rent free in my mind all day. Being able to see through cracks in the floor was not reassuring. I can remember seeing the charred remains of a man, wearing civilian clothing, on the floor in a recruiting office. The upper portion of his body was inside the office and the lower half remained in the charred hallway and was almost nonexistent—a grim reminder of how quickly the fire had moved through the structure. Pictures in the office were still visible but noticeably damaged by the heat and smoke. The man's wallet was laying on the ground. I picked it up, wallets are significant, and put it on the desk so it could go back to the family and not be lost in the rubble. We exited and I'm sure we notified the appropriate personnel, although I can't remember anything but the man and his wallet in great detail. My memory since these events is admittedly crippled. I can remember events of great stress in detail and everyday events are lost on me. I can't remember how many days we were worked at the Pentagon site. I can't even narrow it down to one week or three. I do remember being rushed out of the building at some point because a fire started causing an evacuation. The news media broadcasted the fire and alerted their watchers that soldiers were inside the building. This did an adequate job of scaring the shit out of my mother and other mothers all over the country, I'm sure. I remember being shown a few parts of the plane as they were passed along. I also remember standing guard in a classified area and dicking around with my soldiers to stay awake. We shadowboxed, rolled around on office chairs, and played the movie game. Never played the movie game? We start with the letter A. Everyone names movies that start with the letter until no one can remember anymore. Good answers are movies we respected or enjoyed. You'd be surprised how many movies we could name for a single letter. Moving along. At some point we transitioned outside for the bulk of our work. We guarded the parking lot that the DEA used to go through evidence from the crash and eventually were tasked with assisting the DEA agents. I watched a beautiful blonde K9 searching for human remains. The DEA did impressive work. They were able to locate the razors used by the terrorists. As part of our assignment to the DEA in that parking lot, we had orders to confiscate and destroy any media devices. Occasionally, a reporter would climb up a fence or stop in the road to take pictures. They were relieved of their equipment and sent away.

Even in this horrible event, there was something pretty comical that occurred. A group of men in suits walked up the sidewalk towards the parking lot, I have no idea where their car was but it had to be parked at least a half-mile away. They approached one of my more seasoned team members, Gonzo, and requested entrance. They were denied. They persisted. Gonzo called me over to back him up and I heard the translator explaining to my soldier that they were Russian and had diplomatic immunity; they had even shown ID cards. They told Gonzo they were going to enter the Pentagon. Before I could respond, or maybe because he noticed me walk up beside him, Gonzo simply took his index finger and drug it across his neck. With that gesture, the conversation was done. The group of Russian men began grumbling to each other in their native tongue and walked away, obviously butt-hurt. As a soldier, Gonzo had been a particularly big pain in my ass that year; but in that moment, I couldn't have been prouder. Immunity be damned.

As the DEA completed their evidence searches, they boxed up the findings and loaded them into white, unmarked Isuzu moving trucks. As the ranking soldier in my team, I was stuck driving. My team was armed, and I was given a paper map with step-by-step instructions. The brakes were so bad I remember them to this day with great distaste. We left the Pentagon, traveled to a secret government warehouse, and unloaded the evidence. The warehouse contained retired presidential limousines, huge items under thick plastic (Probably spaceships), and I'm sure the Ark of the Covenant from *Raiders of the Lost Ark*, but we didn't see it. Damn you, high mil plastic!

That same day, we were treated with a quick visit to the DEA headquarters in Pentagon City. The agent gave us some DEA shirts to wear while we transported evidence. I felt like I was cheating on the Army while I wore it, but seeing the envy in a few battle buddies' eyes made it bearable. On another occasion, we folded an American flag on the grounds just outside, surrounded by soldiers of Bravo Company. It was a combined team thrown together for the occasion. I performed the position referred to as "Drag Man," because in a funeral I would have been the person to walk up behind the hearse and drag the casket out for the team to secure. I can't recall being asked to do it, or volunteering. In fact, my memory is so damaged, that until I saw the picture years later, I didn't realize I'd done it at all. Funny how the mind works... or refuses to work.

Towards the end of our participation in what would be later called Operation Noble Eagle, we took a company photo in front of the crash site. I remember this clearly because I almost broke ranks and walked away. I didn't want to be associated with a photo showing our work at the crash site of a terrorist attack. Fucking disrespectful, in my opinion. I understand the need for works such as these, and so I agreed to share my story. I just hate that I was there, that America suffered a blow, that we couldn't defend the nation's capital like the video said many years before.

On September 11, 2001, I'd already turned in paperwork to reenlist in the military. I had points for E-6 and I was waiting on confirmation of a duty station to swear my life away for the next four years. Most of my team had no idea I was going to change my MOS and go to work on watercraft in either Florida or Hawaii. I thought it would be a skill I could apply after the military and the idea of being stationed at the beach sounded like heaven to me. September 11 changed my plans. Well, more specifically, the military did. Because I was a Sergeant in a combat MOS, I was blocked from changing jobs. So within only a few months of my ETS date, I had two options: Go home or go to Korea, leaving my wife and daughter behind. I couldn't bear the idea of being so far from home, with the possibility of another attack in the back of my mind. So, I took my young family back to North Carolina. I took a job chroming motorcycle parts and eventually took a job catching shoplifters while I tried to get my life back on track. I can't remember a lot about those following years because I was dealing with some undiagnosed repercussions of the 9/11 attack. My son was born, my Bam-Bam. I named him after X-men's Wolverine—Logan. I eventually got a job with promise working at a State Prison where I quickly made the Prison Emergency Response Team and became a K9 officer for the Great State of North Carolina.

Like 115 percent of Law Enforcement professionals, I got divorced. I hunted fugitives for the state with my trusty Bloodhound and searched prisons and aircraft for drugs. I trained the state's first Cell Phone detector dog "Bolo." I've saved lives, found missing persons, and caught everyone that escaped from prison in Western North Carolina during my 12-year run. In 2014, a K9 officer friend was killed in an ambush that nearly took my own life, which rekindled some old emotions. I sought counseling from a trusted friend and counselor. With his help and the help of my current wife and love of my life, Tammy, I redirected my purpose to helping kids. That path has landed me as a volunteer with at-risk teenagers and working for the Department of Social Services, Child Welfare Division. Together, Tammy and I have five beautiful, healthy children. I enjoy hunting, dogs, cigars, and riding around in my jeep with the top down.

To all of my Battlehard brothers, I love you and I'm a better person for having known you all.

Operation Noble Eagle

Dennis Brady

Life before the Army? It's so long ago now; it's mostly just stories I tell my daughter to confirm her suspicions that, between her parents, I was the unruly one. I was actually pretty much a derelict. I grew up in the Mat-Su Valley of Alaska, a huge swath of wilderness with a few small towns as punctuation points. I say I'm from the Valley because I split most of my time there between two towns, Willow and Wasilla, but there were also times when I lived in and out of my car or crashed with friends. My dad was a World War II vet who died when I was young, and Mom had her hands full with two boys who didn't get along, to put it lightly. I had little adult guidance and mostly wanted to avoid my older brother, so I spent most of my free time in the woods, riding my bike or walking the railroad tracks to go fishing, camping, or just exploring. I played several sports, being pretty adept at all of them, but not amazing at any of them. My Father left behind a gun cabinet full of rifles, and I was fascinated with them. I was eight years old the first time I ever fired one, and I was hooked immediately. There's something so satisfying about taking aim at a target, squeezing the trigger, and watching a can jump into the air, or a bottle explode. I dreamt of being a Soldier, and carrying a rifle as a profession, but by the time I turned 18 I was in the wrong crowd, and too busy partying to stop and think about what I wanted to be. I worked in various construction fields, then ended up a carpenter after moving to upstate New York. The move followed a marriage that happened way too young; I was 20 and she was 17. We moved so she could go to school there and struggled mightily. After three years of poverty, things fell apart, and I decided to follow my heart and join the military.

My old judo sensei was a former Marine, and I had a ton of respect for him, so I decided to join the Marine Corps. I opened up the Yellow Pages and called the USMC Recruiting Office. Nobody answered. I left a message saying I was interested in joining the Corps, and then I waited. Nobody called back, so I called the second Recruiting Office listed; but, again, nobody answered the phone. I left another message and waited some more. Again, nobody called me back. Shortly after that I was at a big Summer Jam party sponsored by a local radio station, and the Marine recruiters were there. They had set up a pull-up bar and a bunch of guys, and some girls, were showing off while the Marines humored them. I waited my turn and stepped up to the bar, turned my palms inward, and did 11 chin-ups. The nearest Marine complimented me on my form, and asked if I'd ever thought of joining the Corps. I told him that as a matter of fact I had, and I was quite interested, so he gave me a card to fill out. I wrote down my number and checked "yes" to the box stating that I would like to be contacted. Again, nobody called. After a day or so, I opened the Yellow Pages and turned to "Recruiters," but this time my finger stopped at the U.S. Army Recruiting Depot in East Greenbush. I called, they answered, and we set up a meeting. I jumped through all the hoops for them, peeing in cups and retaking the ASVAB. In the meantime, my truck broke down and I couldn't make it to work for a couple days, so I got fired. With no job, I couldn't pay the rent, and I was given an eviction notice.

My recruiter thought I should be an Engineer, because I was already a carpenter and knew how to build things, but I didn't want to join the Army to do what I was already doing. I wanted to do something special, and if I got to fire machine guns, all the better! I thought about being a Medic or a Scout, but there were no training cycles starting before the end of the month, when I had to be out of my apartment. The Career Counselor smirked a little when he told me there was an Infantry Basic Training Class starting in just over a week, and that was all it took. The day before I left, the Marines finally called and tried to give me their pitch. I actually laughed and told the guy he was too late. It seems that God wanted me to be an Army Infantryman.

I had turned 24 the month before reporting to Basic. It was about six years later than I had always seen myself doing this, but I was motivated. I knew how to work hard, and I'd spent the better part of the last year getting into shape, so the level of physical activity wasn't a huge shock. My notion of what Basic would be like was almost entirely based on the movie *Full Metal Jacket*, and anything less intense was going to be a disappointment. I was so pumped when I got there that I was ready to tear the walls down; I was all in. The first night, our Drill Sergeant (DS) came into the barracks blowing a whistle and yelling that we were to wash our nasty asses, and that we would have 30 seconds each to do it. He yelled at us to line up with our brown Army towels folded in half in our left hand while wearing only our shower shoes and PT Shirts. At least I thought he said shirts; it didn't make sense, but I wasn't going to ask for clarification, I was going to follow orders, damnit. I grabbed my towel in my left hand and threw my shorts on my bunk with my right and hustled over to get in line for the showers. I quickly realized that I had misunderstood our instructions, as I took my place, naked from the waist down, between my shirtless platoonmates. That SNAFU aside, Basic turned out to be pretty awesome for me. My DS was too busy screaming and blowing his whistle to notice that I was out of uniform that first night, and after that I was on point. I was never the fastest, strongest, or smartest, but I was usually near the front of everything we did, and I was there to work. The DS must have noticed this, because he put me in charge of the platoon and left me there for the entire training cycle.

We were standing in line for chow one day at the beginning of the cycle, and I saw a guy come walking by in a sharp looking blue uniform. I had never seen the uniform before, and they guy wearing it was tall and fit, and walked with his shoulders back like he was *somebody*. I didn't know who the hell he was, but he stood out in a sea of sweaty, smelly Privates in rumpled fatigues. I thought he was a General, or maybe a pilot, or someone else special. Not too long after, several of us Privates were called into a meeting. I was pretty sure we were going to get smoked for something or other, but that never happened. Instead, the "Pilot General" strode into the room, and I noticed for the first time that he was wearing Sergeant stripes on his arm. He told us that he was a recruiter for the Old Guard (TOG), and he invited us to come join his unit. I had no idea what TOG was or did, but the Sergeant explained everything and answered all my questions. He placed a lot of emphasis on how great it was to be stationed in Washington, D.C., and on how much the ladies like dudes in dress blues. That all sounded fine to me, but mostly I was interested in doing something special that I couldn't do anywhere else, so I signed on the dotted line. The rest of Basic Training flew by for me. I continued to put max effort into everything I did, and I had a good relationship with all the Drill Sergeants. I took in all the information we were taught like I never had in school, and when we graduated, I felt ready to fight with anybody.

I was supposed to report to my recruiting station the next day for Hometown Recruiting duty, which was intended to introduce the recruiters to local high school students. This is probably effective if you are a recent high school graduate, but I wasn't, and my life was a bad country song. The wife done left me, my truck broke down, and I had been evicted from my apartment just before leaving for basic. For all intents and purposes, I was homeless. The recruiters figured I'd be no help to them, so they sent me to D.C. to join my unit. Marshall Codd was the first guy I met there, and he escorted me over to B (Bravo) Company. There was some argument over whether I should be in First Platoon because I'm 6'2" or in Second Platoon because I was over 200 pounds. I didn't know any difference, but there were more Second Platoon guys there making noise, so I ended up going with them. The first couple of months were spent in-processing, partying, going through the Regimental Orientation Program (ROP), partying, learning where I fit into our ceremonial duties, and partying. TOG at the time was a lot like a frat. We were a bunch of rowdy young dudes looking for a good time out in D.C. and sweating out beer the next day. It was the end of 1999, and the nation's biggest fear was Y2K. We were a peacetime Army, and only the oldest and most seasoned Soldiers in B Co. had ever been involved in armed conflict. A few had been in Desert Storm, a few more in the invasion of Panama.

On September 11, 2001, Marshall and I were in the off-post room getting ready for training. We were prepping our riot gear because the International Monetary Fund was coming to D.C., and there were huge protests every time they came to town. The Old Guard had never been called into action as a counter-protest force (at least not that I knew of); in fact, the only action my riot shield had seen was when I used it as a sled during a blizzard the winter prior. We had the radio on as we were organizing our gear, and we heard the news right away that a plane had flown into the World Trade Center (WTC). We were both pretty shocked by that, and we acknowledged that this could be either a tragic accident or a devious attack. When the second plane hit shortly after the first, there was no doubt that we were under attack by someone. I had heard of Osama Bin Laden, but he was not a household name, and so the scope and purpose of this event was still not clear at that moment. One thing that was clear, if some assholes had gone to the trouble of hijacking two planes and flying them into the WTC, it was likely that another one might be coming to D.C. Marshall and I put our gear away and headed downstairs to check in with our leadership.

When we got downstairs it was absolutely bustling. There must have been a platoon of guys jammed around the TV watching CNN. They were showing the WTC burning, and one of our Lieutenants was standing next to the TV like a weatherman, pointing at the smoking hole in the tower, saying, "Everybody from here up is DEAD!" Somebody in the room replied "Yeah, no shit, Sir." Then the LT pretty much shut up and watched. You might expect that an officer would have been barking orders, preparing his men for battle, or preparing them for something. But he was a Lieutenant and a young man (younger than I was), and he was as stunned as the rest of us. It wasn't long before we got word the Pentagon had been hit, and we knew we were directly involved in this.

We waited for orders, and eventually they came. We would all stay at the company that night, spending shifts guarding the barracks, base, and cemetery. In hindsight, the regimental commander (RCO) and his staff must have been as uncertain as any of us. After all, the RCO was a Colonel, and his boss was the Commanding General of the Military District of Washington (MDW), who might well have been in the Pentagon that day. It is not unlikely that the RCO himself was waiting on orders, so we did what is instinctual for infantrymen. We set up a defensive perimeter and faced out.

In the meantime, we were told to go to chow. Even though nobody was able to get in touch with family due to the cell networks all being busy, somehow I managed to arrange lunch with my girlfriend, Margaret, in Georgetown. I was pissed, and already had it in mind to request a transfer to whichever unit was going to be the first downrange in response to the attack. The drive through Georgetown was surreal, like something out of a movie. There were Humvees all over M Street, with National Guardsmen pulling security. After lunch, I made it quickly back across the Key Bridge, then hit the massive back-up at the gate. Prior to that day, I had never seen a single car searched, you only needed to have the base decal displayed on your windshield and they would wave you through. But that day, 100 percent of vehicles were being searched, and traffic was at a complete standstill as the understrength MPs struggled to handle this new task. I couldn't stand to listen to the radio reporting on the damage in NYC and D.C. and speculating on who was behind it. I changed the channel and changed it again. Everything on the radio sucked. Everything made me angry. I tried a CD that someone left in my truck months earlier. It was Hank Williams, Jr.'s Greatest Hits, and it was perfect. That CD played on loop for the next six months.

While B Co. was waiting on orders and pulling security, just a couple miles away the scene was much different. I didn't meet him until years later, when we were assigned to the same unit, but Kris Sorensen was a lab technician at DiLorenzo Clinic inside the Pentagon on 9/11. DiLorenzo is located nearly at the easternmost point of the Pentagon, almost exactly opposite from where the plane struck the building. The Pentagon is a massive structure which covers the equivalent of several city blocks, so the impact wasn't felt in the clinic. Oddly, the staff there watched the same coverage of the news that B Co. was watching in our day room, but they didn't have to wait so long for orders. The staff at the clinic regularly keeps radios on hand to respond to emergencies in the Pentagon, usually somebody feeling chest pain due to the crushing stress of working in our nation's military headquarters, but that day they got the call for all of their emergency personnel to report. This was definitely unusual, and when Kris reported to his designated rendezvous point, he asked if they had two emergencies. Instead, he was told that they were evacuating the Pentagon.

They set about shutting down the clinic and evacuating all the patients who were there. Most were there for routine reasons, some of them in the lab still giving urine samples when they were hurried out of the clinic and into the North Parking Lot. Kris still didn't know exactly what had happened, but when he saw someone in front of him looking over his shoulder with a shocked expression on his face, Kris looked back and saw the smoke rising from the far side of the building. Then somebody bumped into him, and Kris noticed the man was bleeding from a head wound, so he rushed him over to where one of the emergency teams was setting up a triage station. Somebody said they needed to go inside, so they formed a team and headed back to the entrance. By that time there was a lot of foot traffic coming towards them, as this was the farthest point from the impact site, and the Emergency Response Team was going against the flow. Initially this wasn't a huge problem, but as they got deeper into the building the smoke became thicker, and the evacuees more panicked. Now they were not simply rushing into heavy foot traffic, but a near stampede as thousands of service members and civilians were literally running for their lives down the choked corridors. Some people saw them moving upstream and attempted to follow them, but Kris and his team told them to turn back, that they didn't want to go where the team was going. Eventually they fought their way to the center court, where many more casualties had already been gathered. A Corporal on one of the emergency teams yelled for help, and Kris joined him. They ran back into the building, still working their way closer to the impact site, and struggling to see through the increasingly dense smoke.

I should reiterate here just how truly massive the Pentagon is. The footprint of the structure covers about 40 acres of land. That's slightly less than 40 football fields, just to put it in perspective. But it's not just the size, it's also the layout. The building is nothing if not a labyrinth of corridors, offices, stairwells, alleyways, and connecting passages. Anybody newly assigned to the Pentagon can expect to get lost several times for at least the first few weeks there. It takes well over an hour to circumnavigate the outermost halls, and a well-meaning shortcut may well lead to a morning of wandering and being late for a meeting. Now add in the ever-thickening smoke, the rush of people trying to escape, and the panic and confusion that comes along with stinging eyes and lungs. Luckily, Kris and those with him were seasoned vets of the Pentagon corridors, having run them many times when they got the call to respond to an emergency. Even now, nearly two decades later, he was able to tell me which corridor, and which ring they ran down to navigate the building. So it shouldn't be so surprising that they managed to make their way to where a couple of doctors were working on a patient. The guy was burned so badly that the only place they could get an IV started was in his foot. His plastic name tape, normally pinned to his shirt, was melted to his chest. They helped to get him as stable as possible and somehow, miraculously, a sergeant from the clinic showed up with one of the golf carts they used in emergencies, and they were able to evacuate him out of the building so he could get to a hospital.

Their team continued to search for more casualties after that and ended up back out in the center courtyard. By that point there was a triage station set up and manned by 5 or 6 people from the clinic, as people continued to filter into the courtyard, either under their own power or being carried. Meanwhile, some MPs showed up and started yelling that another plane was inbound, and they needed to evacuate the courtyard. Everybody left except the medical personnel and the casualties. The MPs told them they only had minutes to evacuate, so the team scrambled to move casualties and supplies, and somehow found their way out to one of the parking lots. By then the team was completely overwhelmed and running low on supplies, so Kris asked the OIC what she needed, then ran back into the Pentagon again, to DiLorenzo Clinic. The place was an apocalyptic scene, completely vacant, with clinical debris strewn all over. There were even shoes on the floor. Kris worked in the lab, and he wasn't familiar with where everything was throughout the entirety of the clinic, so he started tearing drawers open and grabbing anything that looked useful—bandages, IVs, oxygen, an entire medical chest—and stacked everything into a wheelchair. When he got back to the North Parking Lot, many casualties were loaded onto stretchers, but no ambulances had arrived yet from the local hospitals, so they loaded as many as possible into privately owned vehicles and evacuated them.

A jet flew low overhead. Everybody jumped, expecting another airliner to come streaking in at any moment, but this was a USAF fighter, patrolling the skies above DC to protect the city from any further attacks. When they got word that no other planes were coming, Kris and a few others, some of whom he didn't know, re-entered the building again. They made their way back to the courtyard where the medics had set up a triage station again. Somebody handed Kris a bottle of water. He must have looked smoked, literally and figuratively, after running through the maze of smoke-filled corridors for several hours. Rather than drinking it, he soaked a borrowed t-shirt with it, wrapped it around his face to protect himself from further smoke inhalation, and went back into the corridors. They continued to work their way closer to the crash site until they found themselves in the alleyway between the E Ring (outermost) and D Ring. The firefighters wouldn't let them go any farther than that. The FBI showed up and started picking up evidence. There was a large hole in the wall of the E Ring, maybe eight feet in diameter. The hole was created when the immense pressure from the blast found a weak spot in the concrete, and on the other side of the wall was the cavern created by the explosion. They waited in the open corridor, staring into the hole and hoping to be able to get inside and look for survivors. They never got the chance. The fire was still burning on the other side of that wall, and they could only get a glimpse of what lay beyond. Occasionally the thick black smoke would waft just right, and they could see daylight through the E Ring and a fire truck sitting in the distant parking lot. When they realized they wouldn't be allowed to go any further, they continued to search the corridors and found their way to the basement. As they scoured the area for any more casualties, they happened upon a couple of officers, looking very relaxed, drinking coffee, and in no apparent distress. It seemed they had happened upon a bunker or something. Eventually, they were called to a meeting with all the medical personnel, and several people were selected to stay onsite and maintain 24-hour operations. Kris, barely able to see or think after having run through miles of Pentagon corridors full of noxious smoke, was released to go home. He immediately fell asleep and reported to DiLorenzo Clinic at 0700 the next morning for another day in the lab, while the fire was still burning on the other side of the Pentagon.

For B Co., most of that day was comparatively uneventful. As Kris was reporting to work the next morning, we got word that we were heading to the Pentagon. Margaret and I had just returned from vacation, and I still had a camera in my backpack, with a little more than a half a roll of film. I was in a huge moral quandary about the camera. I felt like it would be disrespectful to those injured, and possibly illegal for me to take pictures of the Pentagon. But at the same time, I recognized the historic importance of that moment, and I felt I had a moral obligation to document it. In the end, I brought the camera, and I've never regretted it. I completed that roll of film and had it developed at a CVS with one-hour developing while I stood by and waited, because I didn't want to lose sight of the film. The next day, there were signs up all over the place expressly forbidding photography of any kind, probably because somebody saw my flash going off the day before, but luckily nobody ever said a word to me about it.

On the evening of the 12th, we loaded up into cargo trucks and drove to the Pentagon. This was my first real Army operation (Operation Noble Eagle), and I was impressed with the organization of what we fell in on. There were tents set up everywhere, there were lights up, and the steady hum of generators. We added our own tent, knowing we were going to be there a while. The whole scene reminded me of a carnival, where you're constantly cutting between tents and stepping over power cords. We were in the grass directly in front of where the jet hit the building. We could see into the crater left by the impact, and into the office spaces left eerily intact on the upper floors. Alpha Company was on duty. We could see them milling around closer to the building, kitted up in Tyvek suits, but they never actually went into the Pentagon because the fire was still burning. When we relieved them there were no more Tyvek suits or other protective gear, so when they finally got the fire out, B Co went in with what protective gear we had, which in this case was our Kevlar helmets and leather gloves. Initially we were given paper dust masks, but eventually someone produced some Home Depot–style respirators, and in we went.

There was a doorway of sorts just left of the collapsed floors. We went

Floodlights and flames illuminate billowing smoke well into the night of September 11 (photograph by Photographer's Mate 2nd Class Lisa Borges, USN).

in through it and entered another world. All the sounds from outside died away instantly. The carnival atmosphere was a million miles away and our new reality was dark and chaotic. Everything was black with soot, and the interior walls had been blown apart, leaving a massive cavern we couldn't see the ends of. There were all types of wreckage thick on the ground, industrial debris, office furniture, computers, filing cabinets, aircraft parts.... And under that was several inches of water and jet fuel. The smell was horrific, and easily penetrated our masks. It was a caustic mix of smoke from burning chemicals and materials that weren't meant to burn, and it lingered in our nostrils and mouths for days afterwards. There was very little light, but we quickly set up work lights to provide better illumination. Someone had gone ahead of us and haphazardly thrown a piece of crime scene tape up, but it was just draped between a couple pieces of debris and was not serving any purpose. An engineer must have gone ahead of us, too, because we had a target to get to: a huge concrete beam, probably 4' × 6' feet, which had cracked clean through. Our task was to clear a path to (and then an area underneath) the broken beam. We did what infantrymen do when stuff needs to be moved—we set up a line and passed things down. There was a loader and dump truck outside taking the debris to the North Parking Lot, but first we had to manually move the debris out. We made slow headway as a couple hours passed, then we were called hastily out of the building. At first, I objected to coming out while there was still work to be done. But the word was that the fire had started back up. Sure enough, there was smoke and flames licking out the top of the building. Codd and I instinctively starting singing "The Roof Is on Fire," then we just as instinctively stopped when we got to the chorus and realized that might be inappropriate. The firefighters got the fire under control, and we went back in. We set our line back up and worked like demons through the rest of the night just to clear a path to the beam. It was daylight when we emerged, and we were all smoked. Nearly everybody fell asleep in the trucks on the short ride back to Fort Myer.

The next night we were issued hard hats, Tyvek suits, rubber masonry boots, and full face respirators. We also wore dishwashing gloves inside work gloves, and we duct taped the hell out of every seam before we went in. We looked like we were sponsored by Home Depot, which is probably where most of that stuff came from. Honestly, we were pretty well set up for protection by the second night. There was also a decontamination station set up by then, and I vaguely recall having to be scrubbed down when I came out of the Pentagon. Funny that wasn't as big of a concern the previous night. Staff Sergeant Delgado (my Squad Leader) managed to cut his finger through his gloves. He stepped out to get a new set so he could keep working, and we didn't see him in the building again that night. It seems there was concern about toxic chemicals or other contaminants, and he required thorough decontamination and wound cleaning. The rest of us continued to work. The task was to clear out an area under another beam so the engineers could shore it up. I grabbed a grain shovel and went to work. I worked like an animal, heaving large shovelfuls of rubble out of the way and just lifting and throwing what wouldn't fit in the shovel. I was possessed, and before we were done, we had cleared a large area under the beam, and it was down to the foundation. By the time we finished, my mask was filled with sweat and I was having a hard time seeing. It was hard work in brutal conditions, but there was nowhere in the world I'd have rather been at that moment.

B Co. worked the overnight shift, and since my sleep pattern was completely disrupted, it felt like I was living through a nightmare. We were working in a veritable hellscape where everything was black and jagged. We waded through jet fuel and industrial debris in search of the dead, and we found them. One morning as we were finishing up, I was lagging behind the platoon, and I decided to wander a bit deeper into the wreckage. There was a path carved out like something from a twisted fairy tale, and I followed it until I came to what I can only describe as a clearing. For reasons I don't know, I stopped in my tracks and just stood there, taking in the scene. There was very little light, and the darkness around me seemed to go on forever. My eyes continued to adjust as I stood there, and eventually a scene unfolded around me. It was like staring at one of those 1990s Magic Eye pictures from the film *Mallrats* where you could see a sailboat from a different perspective. Except it wasn't a sailboat, it was an office. Furniture, desks and file cabinets, blackened with soot were scattered around me, some still upright. Then a desk chair, and a man in the chair. He was wearing a Navy uniform, a Commander. The whole scene became immediately clear, and I saw he was not alone. There were two others with him, frozen in the moment of their death. The man in the chair was missing a hand, but his watch was still on. There was an Ensign lying on the floor behind a filing cabinet, and a civilian woman still sitting in her chair, doubled over and clutching her knees as you would expect someone to do on a plane about to crash. Her ID badge hung on a lanyard around her neck, with her name and photo facing out. I was glad I couldn't see her face, because she looked like she was a really nice person in her ID photo, and I preferred to imagine her that way. If there was a thought in my head at that moment, it was only that they all certainly died immediately. They didn't even have time to get out of their chairs. There was nothing for me to do, so I turned back and headed for the exit. Sometime after that, a wall was erected outside the building, near the perimeter of our hasty encampment. The wall came to be decorated with letters from the family members of the victims in the Pentagon and other supporters. Walking past the wall one day, I stopped and turned to read one of the letters. It was one of hundreds, but the one I stopped at happened to be from the civilian woman's family. I've often reflected on that and wondered how or why I happened upon her and the letter from her family. I've wondered if I should look them up, but what the hell would I say?

After going home one of those first mornings, I woke up after about an hour of sleep. It was probably about 1000 hours. I don't remember having dreams or anything, I just remember waking up PISSED OFF. I was absolutely enraged about the whole situation. I punched a hole in my bathroom door, then called Delgado to tell him I wanted to transfer to a combat unit. I wanted to kill everybody responsible for this mess. Amazingly, he answered his phone. He heard me out for a minute, then groggily said "Brady, go the fuck to sleep. We'll talk tonight." This was no good for me, so I jumped in my truck and drove as fast as I possibly could onto Fort Myer. I wanted to talk to somebody, anybody, about getting into combat. I remember thinking at the time that I was acting completely insane, just totally irrational, but I didn't care. I kept on going until I got to the barracks, which were of course, deserted. I ran to the chaplain's office, but his door was locked too. Fort Myer was a ghost town, because everybody was either at the Pentagon, or sleeping. I wasn't sleeping, so I did the next best thing I could do to speed my way to combat, I went to Clothing Sales and spent about $300 on gear so I'd be ready when I got to my next duty station. Delgado must've told our 1SG about our phone call, because he approached me in the North Parking Lot later that night. He gave the advice of an old veteran and told me to be patient. If I wanted to fight, there was no doubt I'd get my chance. He really talked me down, and he was right, but I've still got the gear I bought that day.

All that time, there were still funerals going on in Arlington National Cemetery (ANC). After a week or so at the Pentagon, it was our turn to rotate back to our standard funeral duty. For a week, we parted with the destruction of the Pentagon and suited back up in our dress blues to pay homage to the fallen. It was a crazy week. We worked harder in the cemetery that week than ever before, adding missions to an already full schedule, but nobody uttered a word of complaint. We knew too well why there were additional missions and we were proud to be part of them. You'd think this might have been a break from the Pentagon, but marching four, five, or six missions per day, standing at attention for hours, and never sitting down is no break. We would finish one ceremony, march off until we were out of sight, get a drink of water, and then march right up to our next funeral. Add to that the surrealism of conducting funerals in Section 68, and there was no escaping it. Section 68 sits at the bottom of ANC, just across S Washington Blvd from the Pentagon. American Airlines Flight 77 had flown right over that spot, flying incredibly low over rush hour traffic seconds before slamming into the western face of the Pentagon. I'll never forget standing at attention, holding the unfolded flag perfectly flat above the Soldier we had just carried to his final rest, while staring across the road into the collapsed floors in the Pentagon where he had died. Beyond the Pentagon, nearly every building visible was draped with a massive American flag. Just a few days prior, I was digging through the wreckage, and just a few weeks prior, this fallen Soldier was walking the endless corridors there while carrying out his duties. Although we were standing like silent statues in our dress uniforms, we were as much a part of the recovery effort in ANC as we were inside the Pentagon.

The remainder of our time at the Pentagon became a little less shocking as the days wore on. Before long, we had manually cleared enough rubble that we could get some Bobcats in there, so most of the removal was done by machine, rather than by hand. We guarded the north parking lot, where the debris was being sifted by the FBI with a few dogs. We were not issued weapons, but we partnered with some local cops who were armed. Ebner and I, armed with flashlights, joked about being like the old Russian army, which had more men than rifles and a philosophy to charge the enemy and look for weapons amongst the fallen as you went. We also guarded the hallways of the Pentagon to keep people from the disaster site, because operations never stopped at the Pentagon. There were hallways that one day might have taken you to your office, but now led to a giant burnt out coffin. Otherwise, we passed our time doing busy work. The engineers would ask for a squad of men to move lumber. Someone else would need men to help transport cargo by truck from one place to another. And on and on...

The rest of Operation Noble Eagle went on like that, and after several weeks, the recovery effort no longer needed a regiment of infantry to keep going, and we were released back to our normal grind. During the invasion of Afghanistan, we took careful note whenever we were burying someone who was KIA over there. I read in the newspaper about a buddy of mine from basic when he was involved in a huge firefight that caught the media's eye. We trained to maintain our skills as infantrymen when we weren't tasked with funerals or other details, and in mid-2003, shortly after the invasion of Iraq, we began to hear whispers of a deployment. It seemed my old 1SG's prediction might actually come true.

TOG hadn't deployed since Vietnam, so it was difficult to believe they would call our number to go downrange. We were considered a non-deployable unit, but the Army was stretched dangerously thin while fighting on two fronts, especially after the cuts to defense spending during the Clinton Administration of the 1990s. B Co. began to spend more time doing tactical training, and less time in ANC. We all heard the rumors of a deployment, but they were just that. Although we asked about it regularly, nobody in our Chain of Command would be straight with us. Eventually it was confirmed that we were deploying, but nobody would say where. One day our company commander told us, after we'd asked about deployment for the 1000th time, "I can't tell you where we're going. I know, but I've been ordered not to say." Within a day of that, the *Washington Post* reported that members of the 3rd U.S. Infantry Regiment (TOG) were deploying to Africa. A day or so later, we were in a briefing with the regimental commander and I asked him if that was accurate. I'll never forget his answer, because it didn't jive with what our CO had just told us. He said, "I can't tell you, because I don't know, and that is the honest to God's truth." We were issued Desert Camouflage Uniforms (DCUs) that day, and several weeks later we were standing on the flight line outside Camp Lemonnier in Djibouti (Horn of Africa). That was my first deployment.

I left the Old Guard and the infantry a few months after coming home from Africa. I met Kris in 2006 when we were both in the same training course. After graduation we ended up assigned to the same company and deployed to Iraq together. I later learned he was awarded the Soldier's Medal—the highest military award for noncombat operations—for heroism during his role in the Pentagon. This never came up in conversation until after he attended an award ceremony for me when I received the same medal in 2007 (under totally different circumstances, which is another story). In truth, we never discussed the specifics of our respective Pentagon experiences until I asked him if he could contribute to this project. Unfortunately, he was not able to due to other obligations, but he gave me permission to tell his story. Reflecting on this, I'm struck with how fate brings us together, and how the impact of our actions often brings about dramatic effects. Of note, the man mentioned above, who needed an IV in his foot, was LTC Brian Birdwell. He recovered from the horrific injuries he sustained on 9/11, retired from the Army in 2004, and went on to be elected to the Texas State Senate in 2010. He has represented the 22nd district (just south of Dallas) of the Lone Star State ever since.

I've changed jobs a couple more times since then, commissioning as an Armor Officer and serving as a Scout Platoon Leader, and later still was accepted into the Interservice Physician Assistant Program. I've deployed to Afghanistan as a PA, and as of writing this, I'm still on active duty, practicing medicine in Korea, less than two years from my planned retirement from the Army. I've seen a lot of changes in that time, in the Army and in our society. Perhaps the most striking to me, given that 9/11 was a defining moment in our nation's recent history, is that nearly all the new Privates joining the Army today were infants in 2001. I've become aware that, very soon, I will meet and train Soldiers who were born after 9/11. That is hard to comprehend. During the middle portion of my career, when the Army was stretched so thin that TOG had to deploy to a combat zone, and the entire Army had to conduct The Surge in Iraq, the vast majority of those serving had joined after 9/11. Their reason for joining was simple, they wanted to fight anybody who would attack us. Regardless of our differences, we had a common purpose in our service. I can't help but wonder what drives this generation to join up, and what will be their defining moment?

A Moment in Time

Larry Carter II

*"Out of the night that covers me,
Black as the pit from pole to pole,
I thank whatever gods may be
For my unconquerable soul."*
—from "Invictus," by William Ernest Henley

As a young man growing up in Lansing, Michigan, I always knew and felt different from others. It was inexplicable like I was destined for something. I was always daydreaming and acting out my dreams, usually, if not always, by myself. This was long before the internet, cell phones, and social media. So, the youth were forced to play outside and interact with each other in those days. I always found myself getting into some type of trouble, some of which was caused by my own hands, some by others. But I also used my hands to help those being picked on or bullied.

I am the oldest of seven children. I will spare the reader the dichotomy of my siblings—just understand they are my brothers and sisters. As the oldest, I was always the responsible one and, in contrast, the one who grew up with the most restrictions. I was always doing some form of chore and was often referred to as the family dishwasher. I used to relish and despise large family get togethers. Seeing my cousins, aunts and uncles was always a joy to my senses, but I loathed the evening events. I was always the one cleaning up after everyone and still do not know why, but it did shape me differently throughout the years. Yes, it made me *responsible*. However, those who did not partake in such labors made me realize the world will walk all over those who do the work. I learned this at an early age, during my preteen years.

As horrible as that sounds, I still love my family and cherish every moment I have with them. Even still to this day, those memories echo through my mind. To be honest, without those experiences I would not be entirely who I am this day. After the Saturday labors of household chores, before noon, I found myself carefree and willing to explore the world I knew and wanted to always take the unbeaten path. I would walk, mainly due to the fact I grew up poor and had no other way, but the only bike I had was stolen from me when I worked at Burger King in the Lansing Mall. That didn't stop my explorative side, the side that to this day exists within me.

College for me was the same. I was still trying to figure myself out and why I was so different. I remember not fitting in entirely with my college football and track teammates, while the one group I was always befriending consisted of those who were outcasts, those who did not conform to societal norms. In hindsight, I am an outcast from those norms, and am proud of it. I did make true friends in college and high school; however, they will all tell you the same—*I am different*!

My very brief professional career before the military followed the same script. It was hard to stay in my cubicle and I found myself always leaving for extended periods of time. My supervisor did not understand my free spirit and that I looked for external things to keep me occupied. Instead of learning who I am, he just wanted to cage me and contain me. I finally grew tired of this type of confinement and decided to listen to Creed's *Higher* and enlist into the United States Army on a Ranger contract. Thus, began my journey. My destiny's door remains fully open.

> "In the fell clutch of circumstance,
> I have not winced nor cried aloud.
> Under the bludgeonings of chance
> My head is bloody, but unbowed."
> —"Invictus"

So, I will spare the reader on what basic training for the Infantry is like and the interesting people involved with its culture. There were funny moments and not-so-fun moments. When a drill sergeant told a recruit to beat their face and the recruit really started to punch their face, the jaws of all those around, including the one who initiated the command, would typically be wide open. To the infamous smoke session during a major tornado storm that turned the sky green. And still we were stuck performing guerilla drills outside. I remember drill sergeants were always trying to push me to act out (which I found funny and disturbing) hoping I would lose my composure. One incident I still laugh at happened during an early morning physical training (PT) session. One drill (short for "drill sergeant") placed his feet under mine while I was in the pushup position and kicked my feet up to flip me over. I just simply started to do pushups again, but he then started to do pushups with me and explained the proper way to perform the exercise. He was still talking when I saw the Colonel walk by. I immediately started smiling and he started to laugh as well as I stated, "Almost got caught!" He simply smiled in acknowledgment.

The IBT (Infantry Basic Training) concluded at the end of the 25-mile forced foot march, which was actually *longer* than 25 miles ... and eventful. The ritual at the end was phenomenal. We were in awe and ready to get to our units to begin serving.

> "Beyond this place of wrath and tears
> Looms but the Horror of the shade,
> And yet the menace of years
> Finds and shall find me unafraid."
> —"Invictus"

September 11, 2001.

The events of that fateful day and morning I do not recall too well; however, memories of the sounds and feelings still haunt me. While holding a team meeting in a soldier's barracks room, the alpha team leader knocked on the door to tell us of a plane hitting the World Trade Center. Moments later, he knocked again to alert us of a second plane hitting and then we heard a loud crash. It shakes me to the core in remembering and writing about that moment. The building was shaking. We all ran outside and saw the fresh black smoke coming from the Pentagon. There were people on the parade field, and everyone looked stunned or in disbelief. I mean this is the United States of America, who would dare attack us at home? It seemed like a movie happening right before our very eyes.

A brief side note: I recall maybe a few months prior a law enforcement agency, which I believe was the Federal Bureau of Investigation (FBI), performing penetration testing in the National Capital Region (NCR) federal facilities. It was determined that the security was too lax and security measures needed to be tightened and updated. I always thought the timing of this to be very interesting.

I remember when I ran to my room, which was in a different building (Echo Company), I made the phone call to my mother to tell her that she probably would not hear from me for a while. I remember her voice telling me to be careful and I felt her words as if she was holding me saying her goodbyes. Words cannot express the fear that was in her voice, as if she knew there was a very real chance she could lose her oldest son! She was very hysterical and crying. No child wants to hear this from their mother. I hear her voice at that moment from time to time and it usually brings a tear to my eye.

At that time, I didn't realize the extent of everything that was going on, but I did recall a recruiter who told me that every 15 years we (meaning the United States) end up in some type of conflict. So, my thoughts raced to that moment with the recruiter as I was making my way back to Bravo Company.

The destruction as seen from above (photograph by PH2 Robert Houlihan, USN).

I remember our first sergeant standing all proud while we were in formation like a majestic peacock. I will say looking back on it as a deployed combat veteran, I would have slapped him for that. It is disgusting to be prideful during a time when innocent lives are being taken. But I digress. As he stood there while we were in the quad, I just recall how he seemed to want this type of thing to happen. Of course, the majority of us had at that point never been in that type of situation, but I expect more from a leader and I will go on the record to say that he and 2nd platoon's platoon leader (PL) were two people who I never wanted to emulate.

The moments from there are a little hazy. I do recall loading up in the deuce-and-a-half (truck) and heading over to the Pentagon to assist in the cleanup effort. As I type this, I am remembering how the company was on lockdown for two weeks. I had a friend at that time coming in to see me via plane. Needless to say, she never made it to see me. Pre–9/11 in the airport, you could walk all around without being screened. I will say that I believe during that time the United States of America had the most lax airport security, if such a thing existed at all.

I remember how we would pull security on the doors of the company with weapons, but we were given no ammunition. Again, the leadership, mainly due to not being exposed to that type of situation, failed the Soldier. We would joke about throwing the unloaded M4s at the airplane if such a thing would occur again. All the while, across the street from the gated section of the base, we would see civilians walking about without a care in the world. I also recall us assisting the base Military Police (MPs) with vehicle screening without us being properly trained, if we were trained at all. The lessons learned from all of this, I fear, will be lost and the cycle will rear its ugly head once more.

I apologize to the reader, as I am reflecting. I am interjecting my professional knowledge of the missteps taken by inexperienced people who were in leadership positions. I encountered the First Sergeant and a PL who I do respect from First Platoon in theater in Iraq a few years later. None of this was mentioned, since we finally saw the bigger picture and understood situations a little better. Experience is the greatest teacher, more so than just reading words in a book.

I do not recall when we were finally on our way to the cleanup effort at the Pentagon, but I do believe we were there for a few weeks. I remember seeing civilians waving the American flag and waving to us as we headed over to the building to assist in recovery and cleanup efforts. Those people showing the American spirit waned over time. I found that to be very disturbing.

I also recall my squad had a flag detail on that fateful day in the same wing where the plane crashed into the building. I will leave the rest for the reader's imagination. Also, before I forget, during my military travels, I have met a lot of people who were affected on a personal level by that day. While I was in Navy Explosive Ordnance Disposal school (NAVSCOLEOD), I met a person who lost their fiancé in the towers. She was left without a future husband and father to their young child. Moments like these pushed me harder to be the best at everything I did.

There were long nights and short days of rest for Bravo Company. We would arrive on the south side of the facility then drop off our gear in tents and go to work. It really amazes me that we accomplished a lot in such short time. Remembering the damage compared to the last part of the two-week cleanup is amazing to me. I do have a memory of meeting General (ret.) Colin Powell's wife and shaking her hand.

The question that still burns in my head is: Why does it seem that Bravo does all the work? That still confuses me to this day.

There were body parts, hands (for some strange reason, I just recall seeing hands) and I heard my fellow soldiers talking about seeing burnt bodies. With seeing things like that, we all said stupid things to make light of the situation we were in. We were focused, however, and ultimately knew we were doing good work. I still have visions of seeing the main part of the plane intact inside the Pentagon. I sometimes wonder if that memory was a part of a strange, weird dream of mine.

At night it seemed is when all the cleanup work was done, due to the strange fact that so-called important people visited the site during the daytime. These visits stalled work from being done and thus we took up the slack in the evening. Since I wanted to be a police officer when I left the service, it did provide an opportunity for me to converse with law enforcement officials when we had a moment or two. I would see a lot of police officers riding ATVs and walking around with their MP5s. I found that very fascinating and was looking toward the future a lot to make the time go by faster.

During a dayshift, I believe it was just First Platoon, we assisted the FBI evidence recovery team with recovering possible pieces of the plane in Arlington National Cemetery (ANC). At that time, I really could not comprehend pieces of the plane being recovered that far away from the point of impact. I do recall finding some fragments however, which taught me the lesson of looking beyond the obvious.

The actual plane was being re-built in the west lot of the Pentagon. It was amazing and creepy to see this, and at night, I would look in amazement at our collective efforts to help solve this forever-changing national event. When we were finally able to resume and return to a somewhat normal life, I would see people taking photos of the hole at the Pentagon while standing on the side of the freeway. The feelings I had concerning my processing of what I was seeing was very mixed at that time. Today I would brush it off;

however, fresh from that incident, I would see people posing in front of the camera with the incident in the background. To me it was distasteful and just poor in execution. With today's social media, I am sure I would get more thumbs-downs then ups for my previous statement.

I felt totally disrespected, as if our efforts were merely for show. I would reflect and ask some of my brethren about it. I do not recall anyone telling me that I was wrong to feel this way. I did recall the country standing behind us and waving flags a few weeks prior. To me, this was a mockery of those who died in that building on that fateful day. Their memory and family's memory of them on display for a few pictures.

Throughout my military and civilian career, I would be reminded of that day and occasionally the sounds from my mother would surface in my mind. I remember coming back to Washington, D.C., from Eglin Air Force Base (AFB) in Florida on a Greyhound bus and meeting the young lady who lost her fiancé that day in New York. Then, as an Explosive Ordnance Disposal (EOD) Technician, I recall seeing a photo of Bravo Company at the Pentagon while we were assisting with the cleanup from a PowerPoint slide presentation from the Alcohol, Tobacco and Firearms (ATF) Post Blast course in Virginia. Then, as a civilian at the Northern Virginia Criminal Justice Training Academy, there was a class dedicated to the events of that day at the Pentagon.

I kept seeing it but tried so hard to forget certain things and managed to do so up to certain points of my life. Then, out of nowhere, the memories would come back because of these moments of training that I subjected myself to. I finally had the courage to speak on these events starting in 2012 as a civilian police officer. As I suspected, they were not received well. I did not glorify the incident, I simply stated how seeing it and doing the unseen work with a bunch of young men changed my viewpoint over time. It amazed me how this event was being viewed and handled by others, particularly those who did not serve or were not present at the Pentagon that day. As I write these moments in my timeline, tears are coming to my eyes showing how upset and hurt I am by these people who probably do not know the pain and sacrifice that day caused others.

My recollection of that day and the followings moments is hazy at best. I pray that the reader was able to see some of the events and situations that occurred during that moment in my life. As stated before, the main memory of that day is the voice of my mother. It was as if I was truly uncertain of the future and was making my last call to my mom. And by the same token, her own uncertainty—Was she receiving the last call from her eldest?

> "It matters not how strait the gate,
> How charged with punishments the scroll,

I am the master of my fate,
I am the captain of my soul."
—"Invictus"

The years after these moments have been very fulfilling and a reflection of that day. I became an Explosive Ordnance Disposal (EOD) Technician, otherwise known as a bomb technician, for the United States Army. I even became a Weapons of Mass Destruction (WMD) Team Leader while stationed at Kirtland Air Force Base (AFB) in Albuquerque, New Mexico. During this time, I have been on one deployment as a team member and I learned a lot during those months. Again, however, I was in Kuwait when I saw an old friend from the Old Guard and even the First Sergeant (1SG) of our company during 9/11. On both occasions, we embraced each other and chatted to catch up but never once did we mention or reference those moments.

There were a few years of respite for me when I was stationed at Kirtland AFB. I was supporting the Department of Energy during this time. There was a lot of personal and professional growth for me that would prepare me for what was to come in my unforeseen future.

When I left there, I went to Officer Candidate School (OCS) at Fort Benning, Georgia, and met a range of people like myself who came from the enlisted side to the officer side to make a difference. One moment really defined me while I was there, and it involved protecting my platoon from being dismissed due to one individual. Needless to say, that individual was kicked out of OCS and we could graduate. After graduation, the Captain who oversaw the platoon while we were in training sought me out in the crowd and told me I would make a good officer. That moment is truly when I knew I was meant to help and protect those around me.

I went on my second deployment as the Platoon Leader for the 789th EOD Company at Fort Benning in 2009 and came back in 2010. Another defining moment happened there that I really do not want to discuss; however, it converted my sureness of my myself to not have the ability to decide if I want to go to the movies or not. I really lost myself for a few years due to a lack of oversight that was not my doing.

I left active duty and trust me when I say my leadership was trying to keep me in. They were really pulling all the stops to do so. Alas, my mind was made up because my heart was broken. I became a police officer in the Washington, D.C., metro area and was immediately reintroduced to the memories and pain of 9/11. There are a lot of people who, in my opinion, truly have selfish reasons to put on a uniform and it manifests in many different forms. I have learned that, no matter what, I must be true to myself and be the leader I am called to be in all situations.

It is still a struggle however, but I am slowly becoming the leader I am called to be, and it is refreshing to have had these challenges in my life to shape me. I am married now to a beautiful woman and have three beautiful, healthy, and outgoing children. Having the fortunate experience of being in the Old Guard and meeting lifelong brothers there (along with the rest of my career in the military and civilian law enforcement) has been a true blessing. Not bad for a kid from Lansing, Michigan!

As I Saw Things

MARSHALL R. CODD

I was born in the Upper Peninsula (UP) of the state of Michigan. I spent my whole life up to age 19 in the town of Bruce Crossing (also in the UP). My upbringing was typical for someone of that blue-collar agrarian region. My friends and I played in the woods pretending to be pioneers or "Army guys" building shelters with hatchets and machetes. Hunting and fishing with fathers, uncles and siblings. We often spent summers working on nearby family farms bailing hay. We had what I would consider to be a large amount of freedom and autonomy, especially compared to today's norms of adult supervision regarding children. And yet, despite spending many summer days miles into the Ottawa National Forest, having crossed rivers and fished for hours along some sunny bank of a muddy stream with no one around, I would return home to find that my mother knew precisely where I had been and what I had done (a trick I have only begun to understand as a parent).

I am the youngest of seven children whose ages span over 20 years between the oldest and me. Being born in 1979 to parents who were 42 and 41 years old, respectively, I believe placed me in the "old school," as I was raised in a more traditional method. We attended church most Sundays and had family dinners where saying grace was a special honor and was observed strictly. No hats on in the house, long hair was frowned upon; almost all my clothes were hand-me-downs and I remember that some of my jeans had patches on the patches. We were, by any measure, poor. But I never knew that, as we always had food and a home (which we were told often to be very grateful for).

Winters in the UP were (and are) famously long and harsh. When I grew up that was certainly the norm rather than the exception. Nevertheless, as a child and teenager, I spent many hours outside sledding, skiing, skating, and quinzhee-building. Not to mention the requisite daily shoveling of the walkway and frequent shoveling of the roof to prevent its collapse, as well as shoveling the driveway to clear the snowbank that the snowplow had built up at the end. My siblings and I were given the honor of doing much of this manual labor. It was sold to us as sort of a rite of passage. Often my father would prescribe a task for us kids which would seem cruel, and if we protested (which was not often, as dissent was met frequently with a spanking) my parents would sternly proclaim that when they were kids they shoveled twice as much in half the time, with inferior equipment under more grueling conditions. They assured me that a little bit of work wouldn't kill me and would even make me strong or "put hair on my chest."

I feel compelled as well to regale anyone reading with the ritualistic time-honored UP tradition of "making wood." This autumn activity entailed going out into the forest with Dad, who, armed with chainsaw and pickup truck, would cut up dead trees into roughly two-foot lengths that would then be picked up by hand and stacked in the bed of the pickup. These were unloaded by hand at home, then brought into the basement—again by hand—and stacked so it could dry and be used for firewood.

Quick aside: burning firewood is still a prevalent method of heating homes in the UP.

I attended the local public school Ewen-Trout Creek Consolidated School District where, again, I had a typical experience for that area. I graduated in a class of 34 students. This was normal and I think lends some insight into the sense of familial community there where "everybody knows everybody." I finished school strong thanks largely to great teachers, great friends who were stronger academically, and parents who emphasized education. I participated in most of the offered extracurricular activities; sports, mostly.

To summarize, my upbringing was tough, fun, and very free. At the age of 18, during my senior year of high school, I decided to join the United States Army in the Delayed Entry Program (DEP). I had a real belief that as a soldier I was defending the country and, indeed, the people and the town I loved so well. I had a strong sense of adventure and the Army seemed to offer everything I felt I needed.

I left home just after my 19th birthday and flew to Fort Benning, Georgia, and reported to the 30th AG Battalion which was a reception and holding station where new soldiers are given their issue, receive their first Army haircuts, and stand in formation for hours doing very little, which I would later realize is a common Army practice. It was there at 30th AG where I was ordered to attend a briefing in the auditorium. The place was packed. A sergeant walked onto the stage and said, "I am going to read a list of things and if any of them apply to you then get up and leave." The list was very long and got more peculiar the longer he read. In that list, and I swear to this, he said, "If you have quote/unquote a 'mortal enemy,' get up and leave." I thought to myself, "What the hell is this briefing about?" At the end of the reading, there were seven people left in the auditorium, including me. We seven were told then that we qualified for the Old Guard. The sergeant showed us a video which looked so cool I agreed to change my orders to be assigned there. The next 19 weeks I spent at Charlie Company, 1/19 learning the art of being an infantryman (11 Bravo or 11B). After that, I spent another three weeks at Delta Company 1/507th Parachute Infantry Regiment (PIR) for Airborne School.

I reported to the 3rd U.S. Infantry Regiment (the Old Guard) on December 24, 1998. Even though I was 150 pounds and very slim, I was put into the casket platoon. I went through the typical indoctrination and the Regimental Orientation Program and decided quickly that this Old Guard thing was for me. I liked the extreme discipline and the prestige that comes with the honor of laying our nation's heroes to rest. I truly believed in the mission of the Old Guard as it pertained to our duties in Arlington National Cemetery.

I will take a moment to recall my arrival to TOG. As I mentioned, I flew in on 24 December, and so most of Fort Myer was dark and quiet, it being Christmas Eve and all. So, I was driven to the Regimental Headquarters building where a sleepy specialist and staff sergeant signed me in and generally gave me a bunch of shit for showing up in civilian clothes despite it being close to eight o'clock at night (2000 hrs). I would learn that giving new soldiers a hard time was not just an Old Guard norm but was common practice pretty much everywhere. Anyway, the specialist drove me in a HMMWV to the Bravo Company building and showed me to my transient barracks room. We made some small talk and when I told him I was from the UP, he perked up because there was, surprisingly, another Yooper in the company. The specialist apparently thought it relevant that we meet and so he took me immediately to another barracks room. The specialist knocked on the door and opened it with the air of familiarity with the occupant. I looked in the room to find it was vastly different than my transient room, complete with a reclining armchair and a minibar in one corner of the room, as well as a large television. The fellow Yooper was sitting in his armchair in a bathrobe or smoking jacket with a bottle of Jägermeister watching *A Christmas Story* on TNN. I think his name was SGT Winger and he was very chill. He offered me a drink of Jaeger which I respectfully declined because I thought it was some sort of trap or test to see if I would engage in underage drinking (I was catching on to the hazing game). SGT Winger told me he intended to watch all 24 hours of *A Christmas Story* and would drink a shot every time it started over. We exchanged some small talk and I eventually bid him a Merry Christmas and went back to my transient room. Based on that encounter alone, I was unsure and concerned as to what the next four years would hold for me. Fortunately, I would learn that it was not generally indicative of business as usual.

Life in the Old Guard

For lack of a more suitable narrative starting point, I will start again with myself and lay out the way I saw things. As I mentioned, I was 19 years old when I joined the Army and was still that age when I arrived at Fort Myer. Coming from a small town the Washington, D.C., environment was totally different than what I was accustomed to. I went from a very small agrarian town to the nation's capital! There were people everywhere ... and I didn't know *any* of them. All the streets and roads were absolutely packed with cars and trucks and bicyclists. My hometown did not have any fast food chain restaurants, but in D.C. they were everywhere and some of them I had never heard of. There were so many things to see and do that the sheer volume of choices paralyzed me (museums, monuments, orchestras, street performances, opera, massive public libraries). As a result of this extreme culture shock, for the first six months I didn't do very much in my free time other than workout (mainly running around the monuments) and going to the movies with my fellow Old Guardsmen. To add even more to this, in 1999 I think that my monthly paycheck was around $1,600; that was more money than I had ever seen in my whole life, so I didn't even know what to do with it at first. I found out that it spent rather easily, and so very quickly.

To help ground myself in this new strange land, I focused on my job and strove earnestly to be the best at it. Whether I reached that goal is not really for me to decide; however, people I respect tell me that I was pretty good. I was a member of Bravo Company, dubbed "Battlehard," in the second platoon (caskets), third squad (Third Herd), led at the time by SSG Giles. The Old Guard was a place that ran and even thrived on strict regimentation and draconian adherence to discipline. It was a fantastic place for a young man because it taught me to value hard work, practice, and attention to detail. The attention to detail part may have been a bit overdone. I say this because a pastime in the Old Guard was to scrutinize one another's uniform. That went on at all times and in all places—even off duty! The result of this constant scrutiny drove me to obsess about my uniform and appearance, but I developed a keen eye as a result and so became rather good in my own turn at noticing the flaws and shortcomings of others' uniforms.

SSG Giles, as I remember, was a quintessential Old Guard NCO. He had a Ranger Tab and was supremely physically fit. My favorite thing to do during morning PT was to try and best him, which gave me a reputation for being a "hard PTer." SSG Giles had a respectable disdain for his soldiers. He was merciless whenever a soldier made a mistake and had very few kind or encouraging words; all the members of his squad feared/respected him. I remember back in those days whenever we got paid there would be an accompanying LES (leave and earnings statement) handed out by Squad Leaders. SSG Giles' version of handing them out was calling out your name and then disdainfully throwing the LES in the air to be caught or land on the floor, he never seemed to care which. Once and only once he handed my LES to me after I earned my EIB (Expert Infantryman Badge) and because he was so stingy with anything that resembled common respect for his troops, that small gesture made me feel as though I was ten feet tall.

As I saw it, everyone in the Old Guard worked hard to be good at their job; however, in any population there is a bottom 10 percent. In our squad that bottom 10 percent was a soldier that I will refer to as Latchy. He was a decent enough fellow, I suppose, but lacked much of the job's requisite attention to detail and was largely socially inept. He also suffered from chronic forgetfulness. As I mentioned, SSG Giles did not possess any sympathy for his best soldiers and certainly had none for Latchy. I suppose some would see this equitable treatment as egalitarian, but it only highlighted to me that Latchy was not someone to emulate. Most of the members of our squad got along enough to work together. Latchy exacerbated his position by seemingly working to be at odds with those around him. He had no friends, as far as I could tell, and either didn't care about having them or had learned to function without them. He was also smelly. I wasn't sure if it was because he didn't bathe or some other glandular reason, but he had his own barracks room and was constantly reprimanded for having a dirty, smelly room. Despite all this, I was happy to have Latchy in the squad because it served as a foil or a sharp contrast between those behaviors that were preferable and those that weren't. Needless to say, Latchy did more corrective pushups than the rest of us.

One time, Latchy showed up to be inspected for a mission in his dress uniform and lined up with the rest of us. SSG Giles performed the inspection, which he did with a precision that rivaled those at The Tomb. For each of us he had a few comments about measurements or press marks etc. When he got to Latchy he told him to go back inside and change his pants because there was a conspicuous stain near the hem on one side. Latchy went back inside and the rest of us "fell-out" onto the bus. Latchy re-emerged from the barracks and joined us on the bus. When we arrived at the gravesite in ANC, we all got off the bus and began reconnoitering the area to decide which path we should take when carrying the casket and where we would march away to be out of the line of sight of the next of kin (NOK). Suddenly we all perked up at the sound of SSG Giles exclaiming his trademark "What the fuck!" which always preceded a dressing down and usually concluded with "fix your shit or I'ma fuck you up, roger?!" Not surprising to the rest of us, we learned he was speaking to Latchy. Apparently, Latchy still had the pants on with the stain that he was ordered to change. When pressed for a reason as to why he disobeyed that order, Latchy is said to have replied "But my other ones were wrinkled."

That excuse may seem perfectly plausible to anyone not intimately familiar with TOG. To us it was not an excuse at all, but perhaps could have been interpreted as a suicide note because it was common knowledge that all uniforms had to be clean and pressed at all times. Nearly every floor of every building on Fort Myer had several large industrial press machines that were available 24/7, and the first lesson at ROP was how to properly press a uniform. If memory serves, Latchy was ordered to have a morning inspection of his entire closet for a week.

I've often been asked if it was depressing to be involved in funerals all the time for my job. I admit the first couple of weeks were difficult. I eventually became acclimated to the routine and focused on doing my best to honor the service member. I sometimes imagined I was at my own funeral as a mental exercise to not focus on the grieving family members.

I can speak only for myself, but I eventually became so inured that I sometimes found it difficult not to laugh or chuckle or smirk during funerals. I realize this is not a flattering admission and it wasn't because I didn't respect the event or the people. The repetition of the job eventually made it so I could perform most of it without deliberate/conscious thought. My mind would wander while standing "on the marks" and sometimes I thought of things that were funny to me. I have heard others say the same thing.

There are, however, certain anecdotes that were funny in and of themselves. I remember one time we were performing a mission at the Columbarium. The Arlington Rep drove up and we removed the remains and the flag as rehearsed and marched to the pedestal. We assumed our positions and unfolded the flag with a precision that only hundreds of hours of practice could achieve. We waited for the NOK to reach their seats. We waited … and waited. Now, it is common practice for Old Guardsmen to wear their hats with the brim low to cover the eyes because it obscures from others what we look at which would take away from the solemnity of the ceremony, and it looks cool. During this mission, my position was the "center catch" position, which enabled me to see the approaching family. I remember I tilted my head back ever so slightly to see what was taking so long. There was a single NOK and she was egregiously obese with an oxygen tank in tow. She would take three or four steps and then stop to catch her breath. It was this slow going and long pausing that prolonged the wait. As you can imagine, seeing this threw me off my game a little. I wasn't an "old dick" yet but wasn't a "recent Richard" either. The fact that it was taking so long for this poor woman to reach her seat gave the mind too much time, and eventually I was biting my tongue hard to stop from outright laughter. I could see from my slightly upturned head that the soldier across from me was looking at me for some clue as to what was going on. I know what it looks like when someone tries not to laugh which is itself funny and infectious. The soldier across from me became comically wide-eyed when the NOK slowly and deliberately struggled to reach her seat that was behind me and so she walked into the opposing field of view from our perspective. What I didn't see (but *did* hear) was that when she attempted to sit down in the green-Astroturf covered folding-chair, she collapsed, and heavily; the chair buckled and she fell out, sort of rolled onto the ground, and then had to be helped up by the chaplain and the Arlington Rep. It is a testament to the ROP training that nobody lost their ceremonial composure that day, but my cheeks and tongue were sore from biting for a few days, as was true of several others.

Those days under SSG Giles' tutelage were very tough but they were nearly everything I thought and dreamed the Army should be from my young, romanticized viewpoint. I may have had a different perspective from Latchy, no doubt, but I don't dwell on that too much because I was successful and was praised, awarded, and promoted quickly. Eventually SSG Giles was moved to another platoon and third squad got a new leader … who was eventually arrested and discharged for spouse abuse. We then got another Squad Leader; he was eventually court-martialed and discharged for polygamy. There were others who came and went under less sensational circumstances; and with their going, so went my naïveté about the world.

I didn't know it at the time, but my tenure in the Old Guard saw a few small but significant changes to that organization and to the Army as a whole. Others and I were regaled often about "the old days" in the 3rd U.S. Infantry Regiment. Before our time, the soldiers, NCOs, and officers had to hand-polish their brass and medals. This was incomprehensible to me because uniform preparation was the most laborious task just with cleaning, pressing, and preening the heavyweight cotton dress blues. To add another layer of skill, the polishing was done on a cotton buffing wheel that required specific abrasive powders and the use of lighter fluid to clean the brass of residue, then wearing immaculate white gloves to apply the brass to the uniform without smudging. This required what I can only imagine as some sort of crippling neurosis or OCD. As well, there was a perceptible cracking down on instances of hazing. It was common practice to make a new soldier march his first mission without socks but instead edge dressing the skin around the ankles. I had the honor to experience this, but the practice died out by the time I was an NCO. Activities like counting the sidewalk stones at a certain memorial or performing the "I'm a little tea-pot" song and dance on the bus for first-mission-soldiers gradually went away because they were seen as cruel. I largely agree that some of the hazing had the potential to go too far and I am not going to quibble. I think of the movie *A Few Good Men* and the contrast between Colonel Jessup played by Jack Nicholson and the lawyer character played by Tom Cruise. The Army was in my time (and is still becoming) a more modern and professional organization, but I feel we lost something in that bargain. When I retired from the Army in 2018, the organization seemed to me wholly dissimilar from 1998. Same mission, same quality of people; better technology and yet somehow diminished. I can't argue with statistics though—we're still successful.

My Recollection of Tuesday September 11, 2001

The morning of September 11 started typically for me. I woke up early and drove to work. I accounted for my soldiers and stood in formation to salute the flag at Reveille. We conducted physical training, ate breakfast, then went about our personal hygiene routines. As a recently promoted Sergeant, I was in the NCO off-post room getting ready to gather my soldiers and start training. In the NCO off-post room there were probably 30 non-commissioned officers; some had small radios, and each was tuned to a different station so that if you walked from one end to the other one could get a smorgasbord of music or radio commentary. I remember one NCO liked to listen to a morning radio "prank" show, so when I walked by and heard something about a plane flying into a tower, I didn't really give it much thought, believing at first it was a prank in poor taste. As I walked towards the door and heard the same thing from another station, I stopped to listen with the other NCOs gathered around. I became a bit more alarmed, went out to find my soldiers, and discovered most of the company was in the dayroom watching the large screen television as the attack unfolded on the Twin Towers. Everyone was enthralled by the footage and, of course, speculation was rampant. Eventually the idea of a terrorist attack became the popular theory, and I remember thinking, "If it is a terrorist attack, why wouldn't they attack the capital?" It seemed just then that news of a plane crashing into the Pentagon came out and the mood in the dayroom changed quickly. All of the NCOs there ordered their soldiers to get to their rooms and prepare for a layout of their "contingency packing list" items. This was, I believe, because no better plan of action at the time presented itself. There were a lot of questions and not a lot of answers, but the command acted to update our records and rosters. A guard was posted at each entrance and we were functionally on lockdown, except to get necessary items from the PX or march to chow in teams or squads.

The rest of the day was spent preparing and waiting. We didn't really know what we were preparing for, but the popular conjecture was that we would be deployed to protect the White House. The entire company spent

Fires raged at the point of impact and deep within the structure for hours (photograph by CPL Jason Ingersoll, USMC).

the night in the Bravo Company Barracks. The NCO off-post room became a bedroom with our sleeping mats and sleeping bags lain on the floor.

The next day was more of the same—updating rosters, layouts, and guard duty. Weapons cleaning, I believe, was also done as a matter of course, perhaps to keep us occupied. I remember there was a lot of anger going around, or maybe frustration. Speaking for myself, I wanted to fight something because I felt powerless. Going back into my journal at the time, I can almost feel the rage in the words that I wrote at that time.

According to my journal entries, on 12 September at 1900, Battlehard was transported to the Pentagon. When we arrived, we established a small base of operations among all the fire trucks and other support and rescue vehicles parked in the grass. At the time we arrived, fires still burned in the Pentagon and fire engines rained water onto the flames. From 2300 to 0400hrs, Bravo Co. had guard duty in an around the Pentagon. We guarded halls and corridors leading to the damaged section of the Pentagon. At 0400, we assembled at our OP and received new orders to put on our helmets and gloves; we would be removing rubble and debris from the building. We formed a line, or a "daisy chain," as we called it, and made our way into the wreckage. From 0400 to 0830, we removed debris so the engineers could shore up the building to prevent further collapse. I recall an official giving us our instructions; he told us to put building wreckage in one pile and plane wreckage in another pile, and if we came across human remains we should stop and call for someone to come and photograph the evidence; then they would responsibly and respectfully remove the remains.

After that, we were transported back to Fort Myer, released to our homes and ordered to return about eight hours later. Upon returning, we performed accountability and returned to the Pentagon to perform guard duty and cleanup operations. We worked through the night replacing a fellow company that worked through the day, and so the effort went for 24 hours at a very high OPTEMPO until 26 September.

There are a few anecdotes I will share, but overall my memory (and even my journal entries) are very general. Some entries in my journal specify hauling lumber and I-beams. Guarding evidence piles, which were basically piles of rubble that were combed through with dogs to look for evidence, and possibly remains.

I remember the rampant "graveyard" humor among the troops at the time. I would guess Bravo Company's soldiers were, on average, 24 years of age, so we were doing whatever we could as young men to cope with some of the terrible sights we saw inside the building. I still shiver a little at the memory of someone putting a shovel into a muddy pile of rubble only to distinctly see, upon lifting it back up, an ear attached to part of a face.

The second day of cleanup was different than the first in that, instead of just putting our helmets and gloves on, we had to go through a series of stations that resulted in us being in full white cleaning suits with full face debris mask, three layers of gloves, and heavy rubber boots. I still wonder what we were exposed to the first day in the Pentagon that might come back to haunt me. At the time, though, I didn't care.

I remember the outpouring of support for the cleanup operation. Businesses donated mountains of food and drinks, clothing, blankets, etc.... I mostly remember the feeling that I was happy that I had something to do to occupy my mind. I believe many people at the time had a feeling of impotence and just wanted to do something, *anything* to contribute.

Life After TOG

In December 2002 I PCS'd from TOG to the Presidio at Monterey, California, in the first step to switching my MOS from Infantry to Military Intelligence. My experiences from 9/11 shocked me and expanded my view of the world. I think the experience presented me with the often-quoted question, "If not me, then who; and if not now, when?" I believed I had the ability, and therefore an obligation, to do more. It was out of this experience that I changed my plan of only serving four years and then going to college. When I re-enlisted, I pretty much knew I would stay in until retirement.

In short, after TOG I changed my MOS to 35P, cryptolinguist. In 2008, I applied for and was selected to attend Warrant Officer Candidate School, changed my MOS again to 351M, and recently retired after a full career in the United States Army.

A Recent Richard's Recollection of His Time Recovering the Pentagon

ERIC EBNER

I moved out of my childhood home sometime in the early summer of 1999. Me and a pal from high school managed to get a little duplex rental house in the bad part of town. We had just graduated from high school a month prior and were determined to make it work. I had held down a job since I was 15 years old and was working at a local supermarket at the time. Our house was close to the local college, which we would be attending in the fall.

The problem with our scheme was that we had not considered the amount of irresponsibility that a couple of under 18-year-old boys can generate when left to their own devices with zero oversight. We threw massive parties that summer. We were the only ones in our group of friends not held in check by the watchful eyes of parents or dormitory RAs, so our place was "The Place." We would pack our half of the duplex with beer, booze, weed, and dozens of people on a regular basis. The only reason we didn't have the cops called on us every other night was that no one called the cops in that neighborhood.

My life at the time was the maddest it ever was or (hopefully) ever will be again. One night, for example, we got raided by the Sheriff's Department while throwing a party. This was a drug task force that had been following one of our friends for some time. This friend (we'll call him Kristoph) had been slinging weed for this mid-level dope distributer that they were trying to take down. They followed Kristoph, observed him coming by our place every day, and concluded that our house was where he stashed his supply. This was not the case. There was plenty of evidence that there had been marijuana in the house, but not the amount they were looking for. The Sheriff's Department detained the 20 or so people at the party, tore through our house, searched our vehicles, and came up with nothing. When it was all said and done, they didn't even say goodbye.

The fall semester at college was a disaster. The State of Louisiana has a tuition program called TOPS. In order to keep TOPS, a student must maintain a GPA of 2.5. I limped through the semester finish line with four classes withdrawn and three classes failed. GPA of 0.0. College was no longer an option for me, but I still had a steady job to fall back on. The funny thing about failure is that it creates a very slippery slope that, if left unchecked, escalates into a spiral.

Failing college created in me an apathy that bordered on insanity and I slipped into a downward spiral quite easily. My job tried to call me in to work on my day off, which ordinarily wouldn't have been a problem. On this day me and some friends were about three hours into a psychedelic head trip. My mental state and perception were sort of skewed at the time, so I don't exactly remember what I said when I quit my job. I can only imagine that my manager was very confused by the end of that conversation. Now jobless, I had to move home to my parents' house.

By the time the summer of 2000 rolled around, I was a cult missionary's dream candidate: disillusioned and lost. When I look back at this time, I have often marveled at how very lucky I am that that there has never been a heavy market for Heaven's Gate or Branch Davidian cult-like organizations in my hometown. I would have fallen directly in step with one of them so very easily at this point.

The only cults we had laying around in Lafayette, Louisiana, had budgets approved by the U.S. Congress and funded by the American taxpayer. The Navy had been trying to recruit me before I had graduated from high school, but I figured that ship had sailed the moment I flunked out of college.

My first stop was at the Army Recruitment Office, where the recruiter regaled me with the multiple advantages to joining the Infantry. He threw an Airborne School contract and a signing bonus into the mix and I was ready to go. By October of 2000, I was in Fort Benning, Georgia. While getting a regimen of shots at 30th AG, a Staff Sergeant pulled me out of line and asked how tall I was. Then he asked what my General Task score on the ASVAB was. It turns out he was the Old Guard recruiter, and it was as simple as that for my path to be directed to Fort Myer, Virginia.

Infantry School was a blur. To me it was a combination of school, prison (not that I'd ever been), and football practice sprinkled in with a large dose of Violence Culture. Once you figure out the routine and push yourself to never quit, it is manageable. Enjoyable, even. I loved it. I slowly but surely purged all the mental walls I had created for myself and I became stronger in body and mind. I started the course weighing 185 and exited at 210 pounds. By the time of graduation, it seemed as if my entire life had been spent there. I have never felt more accomplished than when my Infantry Crossed Rifles were pinned to my chest.

After a brief holdover period, I started Airborne School. There isn't too much to say about it other than it was painful and exhilarating. I was bathing my legs, shoulders, and back in Icy Hot every night just to keep going. I made my five jumps to get parachutist-qualified and went home for a brief leave period.

I reported to Fort Myer, Virginia, on April 16, 2001. I was assigned to Bravo Company and escorted to the company by the Regiment Staff Duty NCO. After getting in-processed, I was sent to 2nd Platoon, 3rd Squad. I later found out that is where the "beefier" guys end up. One of the Team Leaders helped me drop off my gear and took me to get introduced to my Squad Leader. Our first conversation:

"Where are you from?"

"Louisiana, SSG."

"So, you got a lot of Klan down there?"

"Roger SSG, but mostly on my mother's side of the family."

Full disclosure: he said "Klan," which I understood as "clan." There is a very distinct, yet subtle, difference here. I have never been looked at in the same fashion as my brand-spanking new squad leader looked me at that moment. I quickly realized my naïve mistake and was worried that he would forever brand me in his mind as being some yokel raised by white cloak–wearing psychopaths. I was later assured that he understood the misunderstanding and didn't think I was raised by the Ku Klux Klan. This was a huge relief.

My transition into the squad went rather smoothly, and I was trained up to do work in the regiment. Second Platoon was tasked with casket-carrying duties in Arlington National Cemetery, and I really enjoyed the job. The summer came and went, and I made friends with a lot of guys in the company from a lot of different parts of the country. I became best Old Guard friends with Platoon mate Monte Swapp, or MJ, during this summer as well.

The summer ended and the crushing heat of Virginia finally started to break. I was used to heat from growing up in Louisiana, but I wasn't wearing heavy woolen dress blues. By the time September rolled around, we were gearing up to train for an event called Spirit of America. It was a show that the Military District of Washington put together as a way for the general public to see what the Old Guard was all about while getting a healthy dose of American patriotic propaganda.

One of the major advantages to living in the barracks was that one always had a place to catch a nap when the opportunity presented itself. After physical training in the morning, I usually found between 20 to 30 minutes to rest and relax after breakfast but before we needed to report for duty. It was during one of these quick naps that I was very loudly awoken by MJ bursting into my room and yelling. "Wake the hell up, man. Some maniacs just crashed some plane in New York! Everyone's in the dayroom, they are talking about maybe getting our riot gear ready!" I thought he was messing with me, so I reached over, grabbed a boot, and chucked it at him. He closed the door to block it, opened it again, and continued: "No, man, I'm serious! We may be drawing weapons! Let's go!"

We made our way down to the packed dayroom just in time for images of the second plane hitting the South Tower to be played on the screen. I'm not remembering if that was the exact moment the second impact was reported or if they were recycling images from a few minutes' prior. I do remember that at that moment SGT Jon Hoffman said, "Well, looks like we're going to war."

Rumors flew around faster than they could be marginally processed. "The Pentagon was hit by a missile." "A plane just hit the White House." "We were drawing weapons." "Multiple bombs had gone off all over Washington D.C." Everything was confusing chatter, but eventually it all quieted down and we had a company formation. Bravo Company leadership established that the Pentagon had been hit as well, and that we would possibly (probably) be involved there in some capacity.

Bravo Company found itself at the Pentagon the night of the 12th. The entire scene was illuminated by generator-powered floodlights, and the gaping maw of the crash site seemed to have collapsed in on itself at some point. The firefighters had put out the fires, and we were going in to clear a path for the engineers. We walked in a single file line and made our way into the remains of the building. The only other time I was as scared as I was during that first walk into the building was each jump at Airborne School. I treated it the same way: shut off your mind, follow the man in front of you, and keep moving.

My first impression of the inside of the building was an image from *Star Wars: A New Hope*. There is a scene in the film where the heroes are making their escape though a chute and end up in a trash heap. The inside of the crash site looked like that trash heap to me: gnarled metal, burnt wood, miscellaneous debris, and water. The smell inside was something I will always remember. Each and every one of my senses received signs of burnt pain and misery. Our NCOs were in the process of getting us organized into a bucket brigade when the call came out that one of the fires had reestablished itself. We got out of there double-quick and regrouped outside while the firefighters addressed the situation. I am not even sure that there was a fire. It may have been simple panic brought on by overwhelming circumstance and generated through the line.

Our time there was a grind, but the time we spent inside the building was carefully regulated by our leadership. We were tasked with working nights, which was a blessing. I've always preferred nights. The air was cooler, and the media presence was far less established. The media can get you in trouble. We heard that one of the guys from one of the Companies working during the day was asked by a reporter, "And what are you guys doing here, exactly?" At that moment, his platoon was on a regulated break from the building and he was resting on his rucksack. His reply: "You're looking at it, lady." We worked throughout the nights performing various tasks. Sometimes we were pulling material out of the building. Other times our job was to man security checkpoints inside the building just outside of the destroyed zones.

Once the lower levels were shored up by the engineers, the debris-clearing operations shifted to upper floors. We had been chucking the remains of office furniture outside of a busted-out window for most of the night when I realized that my birthday had come and gone. I turned 21 years old inside the remains of what was supposed to be some Pentagon office, wearing a respirator and Tyvek suit. Once we knocked off that morning and got back to the barracks, Montimur and I walked to the Class 6 and I legally purchased a bottle of Jack Daniel's. We got back to my barracks room, took a shot of whiskey each, and retired to our respective rooms to rest up for the upcoming night. Sometimes people have crazy stories about the night they can legally drink. They have tales of debauchery, drunkenness, bad decisions. I have become more partial to mine as I grow older.

Once the emergency recovery effort was approaching completion, we transitioned over to working days. Me and Specialist Brady were tasked out to the DEA to provide security and assist with moving items from the crash site to some warehouse in DC where investigators had amassed all the evidence. It was a large room with tables run parallel all the way across and down. The tables were labeled: "Possible Terrorist Items," "Flight Crew Items," "Building Effects," "Passenger Items," etc. We were tasked out to this DEA guy for a day and then rejoined the Platoon.

I sometimes bring up that story when I am confronted with someone who subscribes to the conspiracy theory that it was a missile that struck the Pentagon. I am well beyond trying to change anyone's mind about the matter, especially someone who has dug their "intellectual" heels in. However, I have learned that it is exceedingly rare for most people to meet someone who was there on the ground in the crash site. I am happy to say that I have been able to redirect the thinking of a few now-former conspiracy theorists out there.

The unofficial term for a new Old Guard soldier was "New Dick." Dennis Brady called this time the "Recent Richard Phase." Having been at the regiment for a mere six months or so, I was definitely still a New Dick when the 'Gon got hit. The only reason that I did not go completely crazy during this event is that the guys I served alongside were there every step of the way. We were all shocked initially, but that shock turned the corner fairly quickly and we were back to the usual shit-talking and joking around in almost no time. One time, we were all packed into the back of a transport truck and about to head back home one morning. The Platoon Sergeants were going from truck to truck to get headcounts for accountability. Our truck had already battened down the canvas back cover, so the Platoon Sergeant from 3rd Platoon was having a difficult time getting a count of us. Frustrated with opening the back, he exclaimed "Hey! How many guys we got back there!" In a high cartoonish voice came the reply from Jon Hoffman: "Nobody here but us chickens!" The entire truck erupted in laughter. I couldn't remember the last time I had laughed so hard. It was one of the best laughs of my life and came at the perfect time.

    Our mission eventually wound down at the crash site and we transitioned into supporting the MPs with the gate security at Fort. Myer. Once that was complete, we moved back into the regular rotation of funeral operations in Arlington. The rest of my time in the Old Guard was a blur, honestly. I was moved to the Full Honors Casket Team, aka 8-Man. In 2003, I was moved back to the Pentagon, this time assigned to the Public Affairs Office to work as a Pentagon Tour Guide. I coasted there for a while, until Bravo Company deployed to the Horn of Africa. We were there until the summer of 2004.

    I had a great experience with leadership from my initial arrival at the Old Guard up until our return from our deployment to Africa. The Platoon Sergeant that we had from the Pentagon Recovery and through deployment to Africa retired. Second Platoon had a new Platoon Sergeant by the time my term of service was winding down in late 2004. This new guy either did not like me or did not care that I was getting out of the Army soon. I was not allowed to attend crucial appointments in a timely manner and was assigned to random work details up until the last minute. Due to restructuring of the squads, I had no viable leadership to go to bat for me. In the end, I was still out-processing the Army four days into my terminal leave. My exit from active duty has always left a bad taste in my mouth, to be sure, but has given me valuable insight of how not to treat people under your care. I've treated my clumsy exit as a learning point and will never hold personal animosity towards Bravo Company as an organization.

    Since my time in B Co., I have worked in a variety of industries. Immediately after active duty, I stuck around the D.C. area and got a job at Home Depot. Matt Genkinger was the guy to get me into the door at the depot. He was in 1st Platoon, so we were never more than really close acquaintances while we were on active duty. We were roommates in Virginia for years afterwards. In 2006, I transitioned over into the irrigation industry while getting back into the Army by way of the 11th PSYOP BN, a Reserve unit. My youngest brother was having a tough time back home in Louisiana. He was running with the wrong sort of crowd and I saw a lot of me at 19 years old in him, so I moved him up to Virginia to live with me and got him a job in irrigation. He was able to get his act together, thankfully, and refers to his move to Virginia as his "Army."

In July of 2007, I was dating a girl who lived in Virginia Beach. I was visiting her and at a Build-A-Bear with her son when Genkinger called my cell phone. He told me, "I'm sorry to have to tell you this, but Fritsche is gone, man." I didn't have a grasp on what he said, and the toy shop was loud with screaming children, so I stepped out of the store and asked that he repeat what he said. Fritsche was one of my 8-Man squad mates. He was one of the best men I ever knew, just genuinely good all around. He was my friend, and he was killed in Kamu, Afghanistan, on July 27, 2007. The last time I was as torn up as I was when learning of his death was when my grandpa died back in 1994. I was inconsolable. At the time of this writing, it was 12 years yesterday that he was KIA, and I still get a bit "emotional." And by this, I mean "weeping shamelessly and without reservation."

I moved back home in the fall of 2009, and started going to college at the same university I had failed out of some 10 years prior. I got involved in the search for a missing woman in the summer of 2012. The example set by Bravo's leadership enabled me to become a focal point in this search operation, which was a mentally and emotionally exhaustive affair.

After graduating in 2013, I hired on with one of the major oilfield service providers as a surface data logger. My main purpose at work was monitoring drilling operations for well control purposes. I did this for six years, working 14 days on/14 days off, and finally burned out in July of 2019. I'm not sure what the next big thing will be, but I know that I'll be able to handle whatever may come my way.

9/11 Revisited

Matt Genkinger

The family farm rested on 200 acres in the rolling hills of southeastern Iowa where, millennia before, glaciers carved out rivers and streams, leaving behind the richest soil on Earth. My ancestors were among the earliest pioneers west of the Mississippi River. Life was incredibly difficult for these intrepid souls. They constructed log cabins and sod houses, using the earth to shield themselves from the oppressive heat of the summer and crippling cold of winter. They used crude tools and beasts of burden to turn the thick prairie grasses into fields of corn and pastures for livestock. They lived peacefully alongside native tribes. Subsequent generations continued improving the land.

By the time I was born, machinery had replaced oxen and horses; semi-trucks came at the harvest to move the abundance of corn and soybean to railyards. Aside from songbirds and the occasional summer thunderstorm, the landscape was perfectly quiet and serenely pleasant, only interrupted by the freight trains hauling seed or coal and the famed "California Zephyr" Amtrak line running along Burlington Northern Rail Line.

The people were as pleasant as the landscape. Old men sat in diners drinking coffee in their overalls and seed-corn hats discussing weather forecasts and the price of a bushel of beans. Stands were packed every Friday night in the fall and church pews full every Sunday. I graduated from the same high school as my great grandfather, although surely the heating had improved somewhat.

All the young men who were able left the farm for a time to serve in the Army. Stories of service among our ancestors reaches all the back to the Revolutionary War. My mother, sister, and nieces are on the rolls of the Daughters of the American Revolution. We learned through genealogy projects conducted by several branches of the family tree that six men on my mother's lineage served during the War of Independence. Seven fought in the War of

1812 to include one who would venture westward. As the Fairfield Ledger memorialized on October 20, 1886, "at Lockridge, occurred the death of John Toothaker, one of the oldest, if not the oldest, citizens of Jefferson County. Mr. Toothaker was a native of Maine, but went to Ohio early in life, and has been a resident of this county since 1843. ... At the time of his death, Mr. Toothaker was 92 years of age, and until recently he had enjoyed very good health and had been able to stand much more work than most persons of his years. He was also one of the few surviving soldiers of the War of 1812." One of his grandsons, Charles Wesley Toothaker, volunteered for service during the Civil War. Assigned to Company M, 4th Cavalry, Iowa Volunteers, he was wounded in Battle of Shiloh. Each generation was called to serve, especially during a time of crisis, as my grandfather did by enlisting in the Army Air Corps after the attack on Pearl Harbor. My great-grandfather on my father's side enlisted in the Iowa National Guard in 1892 as a cavalryman. Interestingly enough, his father emigrated to the United States in order to avoid conscripted service, but a cavalryman in the National Guard was charged with the full-time duty of caring for this issued horse which came in handy for a poor farmer. His—my grandfather—and grandson—my dad—would also serve in the National Guard. My brother enlisted just after Desert Storm and is a veteran of the conflict in Somalia in 1993 and the wars in Iraq and Afghanistan. As fate would have it, I would also enlist in the Army. Little did I know of the history I would experience.

I left Iowa in 1999, just shy of my 19th birthday and a few months after high school graduation. A quip I often use these days when folks ask if I served is, "I joined for the college money and stayed to kill terrorists." Like all or most of the contributors to this effort, I attended basic and advanced individual training at Fort Benning, Georgia. Upon graduation and a brief reunion with my parents, I reported to the 3rd U.S. Infantry Regiment ("the Old Guard") at Fort Myer, Virginia, on January 2, 2000.

The first year of my time in the Old Guard was quite a blur. We participated in a rotation to the Joint Readiness Training Center, celebrated the 50th Anniversary of the Korean War, executed hundreds of funerals in Arlington National Cemetery, retired several general officers, and participated in several "Twilight Tattoo" ceremonies on the ellipse of the White House. I had even been selected to participate in a mass-casualty exercise at the Pentagon in the fall of 2000—on a Saturday, no less. Aside from all the "fun" stuff, we remained as tactically proficient as possible, busing down to Fort A.P. Hill for weapon qualifications, land navigation, squad-level training, and normal infantry tasks. This was, from my understanding, how the four-year enlistment would go.

As a newly promoted Private First Class (PFC), I happened to have broken my wrist during a training accident in January of 2001. After "riding the

CQ (Charge of Quarters) desk" for a couple of months—as most guys rehabilitating from injuries were required to do so the unit's mission could carry on—our company executive officer (XO) approached my platoon leadership to help the headquarters platoon prepare for an intense inspection. Upon reassignment and attending several two-week courses, I became the company's Communications Non-Commissioned Officer and the Nuclear, Biological, and Chemical (NBC) Non-Commissioned Officer. Along with those duties came another—the company commander's (CO's) driver.

On September 11, 2001, I was working in the NBC office preparing for an inventory of spare parts for gas masks. To break up the silence, I had the radio tuned to a local station with a popular morning show. Around 0900hrs, the first reports of a plane flying into the World Trade Center in New York came over the airwaves. I immediately recalled an event from 1994 in which a stolen Cessna had been piloted to crash on the White House lawn. Assuming this to be the case, I went back to the task at hand as the radio personality resumed his programming. As fate would have it, the situation in New York was much more catastrophic. The shock jock host interrupted his set yet again to announce the second plane hitting the World Trade Center, in more graphic detail. I stopped what I was doing and ran to the only place where I knew there to be a television. There, gathered around with several other guys who had heard the news, we watched in horror as smoke poured out of both buildings. In that moment, we realized our country was under attack. I clearly recall one of the guys saying aloud, "They're gonna hit D.C. next."

At 0937hrs, the Pentagon was attacked. I can't remember exactly where I was at that moment and maybe as the years have gone by, I've convinced myself that I could hear that plane flying low and fast through Arlington and could feel the impact of that jet striking the Pentagon. Perhaps the imagery from cable news has replaced my own memories of that moment. I distinctly recall being in the NBC office with the door closed hearing our first sergeant (1SG) yell down the hall, "Men, prepare for war!"

The unsettling feeling I recall at that moment will stay with me forever. After all, I had enlisted in the Army as an infantryman. We are the professional bullet-catchers.

I readied the remaining M40 Field Protective Masks for those who hadn't been issued one and loaded the cryptologic codes into the Single Channel Ground and Airborne Radio Systems. In the hallway outside, soldiers lined up in front of the arms room to turn in their ceremonial Vietnam-era M14 rifles for M16A2 rifles.

The XO came into my office to provide an update. The CO had received a call from the regiment. He was to go to the Pentagon for a leader's recon and I was the only person in the headquarters platoon with a valid military driver's license. I locked my door and followed him to his privately-owned vehicle with all of the proper dispatch paperwork for one of the two HMMWVs the company stored at the regimental motor pool. Looking out the window as the XO drove down the steep slope of Jackson Avenue (also know as Cardiac Hill), I could see the smoke rising above the treetops of Arlington National Cemetery coming from the chaotic scene of the Pentagon.

Dispatching the HMMWV proved easier this day. Usually, the dispatcher, one of the regiment's mechanics—typically a PFC or specialist—would give you a hard time while conducting an inspection of a vehicle. One might hear a dispatcher quip, "You need to top off your brake light fluid before you bring it back, or I won't take it back." Instead, he was quite helpful and informed us of the base closure (the military police had already been by to dispatch their vehicles and let the poor kid know he couldn't go off-post for lunch). The HMMWV cranked to life. We affixed the radios to their mounts, conducted a test with an operator at Regimental Headquarters, removed the blocks from the tires, secured the drip pan in the back, and roared back up the hill.

While we were away, the company 1SG had established security at every entrance to the building—which doubled both as a headquarters and barracks for those who lived on-post. Guards were wearing issued riot gear equipment and carrying M16A2 rifles with an empty magazine. It seemed a little absurd at the time, as it wasn't clear to me there was a threat from within. And had there been, the first target would surely be a softer civilian target. Yet, here were a bunch of guys standing at the doors, ready to deter anyone from entering the building.

A small access road and eight-foot chain-link fence with barbed wire atop separated our building from U.S. Highway 50 in Arlington. During rush hour, "Route 50"—as it is commonly known—is a grind of commuter cars, buses, and taxi cabs slogging suburban dwellers into and from the city for work. On this day, traffic was stopped in both directions. I recall someone spreading a rumor of the Virginia State Police closing Interstate 66, the only alternative to Route 50, due to the attack. Emergency vehicle sirens blared out over the stalled traffic in a futile attempt to navigate through to the Pentagon.

After changing into "full battle rattle" (Kevlar helmet, load-bearing equipment, bulletproof vest, protective mask, and M16A2 rifle) I returned to the HMMWV to wait for the CO. Waiting there in the vehicle, the gravity of situation began to sink in, and questions began racing through my mind. "How could something like happen? With our significant military might, who would do this? How many people have been killed and hurt?" I thought to call my family, but the call would have to wait until we returned.

The passenger door opened and the CO clambered into the HMMWV.

He, too, was adorned in issued personal protective equipment and he wasn't happy about it. "I'm carrying the [expletive] M16 without any rounds! What am I gonna do with this damn thing? Beat someone with it? Aight, let's roll." He grabbed the handheld microphone and spoke into it, "TOG, this Battlehard 6. Moving to rally point." Someone responded back and with a nod, I put the transmission into drive.

He pointed out where to go until we came upon several other HMMWVs parked in front of Old Post Chapel. Here, on any other Tuesday, one would usually see a horse-drawn caisson, crisp-dressed service members, and an Armed Services band gathered in front of the chapel conducting a full honors funeral for a recently passed veteran. But on this Tuesday, parked in front of the closed gate to Arlington National Cemetery was a Fort Myer Military Police patrol car. The CO got out and met with the Regimental Commanding Officer (RCO) and presumably commanders of the other infantry companies stationed on Fort Myer at the time. The RCO must have been briefing the men on the situation down at the Pentagon along with other pertinent details such as the risk for follow-on attacks, primary and alternate routes back, etc. My mind flashed to a book I had recently read in which a military convoy was targeted for attack while conducting rescue-and-recovery operations in Somalia in 1993. Shortly thereafter, the book had been made into a movie, *Blackhawk Down*.

The group of men broke their huddle and returned to the trucks. The CO clambered back into the now very hot HMMWV. He said we'd be going down to do a site survey of the Pentagon, going through ANC. I was instructed not to follow the vehicle in front of me too closely. We rolled through the serene landscape of the cemetery, past all the white headstones. I recall seeing a vault company digging a new grave as we approached Section 60. "Do those guys realize there will be no funerals conducted today?" I wondered.

Part of the Pentagon was now in sight. I could see black smoke billowing over the trees. We turned into the service complex of Arlington along Patton Drive and another Fort Myer Military Police car pulled away from the exit onto Columbia Pike. Going against traffic, our convoy weaved between vehicles parked and abandoned on the exit to Washington Boulevard, a bifurcated expressway along the south of the Pentagon. There, finally, we witnessed the destruction of radicalized Islamic terrorists against the heart and brain of our great nation's defenses.

Our convoy came to a halt. The CO stepped out and yelled "stay here" as he rallied with the other commanding officers. The impacted area was over my right shoulder, and anyone who has been behind the wheel of a HMMWV knows you cannot see another in that vast blind spot. Looking out the windshield, I could see emergency vehicles lined up around the cars left on the

The Pentagon's impact-damaged area set ablaze by jet fuel (photograph by CPL Jason Ingersoll, USMC).

road. Police, firefighters, civilians and service members of every branch were watching all that was happening while resting on the guardrails of the highway. I recall seeing fighter jets flying high above coming from the Rosslyn area and helicopters which I presumed to be from the local news channels flying about.

Before I could really take anything else in, the CO returned to the truck and we headed down Washington Boulevard back towards Fort Myer, going against the non-stop traffic. It was a very quiet ride. I didn't ask any questions and the captain didn't have anything to say until we approached the gate to Fort Myer. "G, call your folks when you get back to the office. It is going to be a long couple of weeks."

We parked the HMMWV in the "quad" of the barracks. I put the drip pan under the truck, chock block behind the tire, and locked up the steering wheel. Returning to my office, I called my mom. "I'm fine. Have you heard from Rob?" My older brother Rob (who was now a reservist in the Army) and I lived in an off-post apartment in Alexandria. He was supposed to be at the Pentagon that day but was instead told to report to another location somewhere in Fairfax. She told me he had called and was fine, but that he'd be stuck out there awhile as the interstate highway—I-66—had been closed to civilian traffic. She was worried about us, of course, and worried that other attacks were imminent. I tried to reassure her I was fine, but I really had no clue. I didn't have much else to say. I recounted to her my trip to the Pentagon with the captain, but had nothing else to share. I hung up the phone and turned my radio back on. It was then I learned of a fourth aircraft that had disappeared somewhere in Pennsylvania. No one was sure where it was at the time and we all braced for another round of attacks.

Evening approached. My turn to stand at the doors arrived. Wearing riot gear and carrying a rifle, I reported to the back stairwell. The guy I was relieving cleared his rifle and handed me his empty magazine. I slapped the magazine into the well of my rifle and may have said something to the effect of, "This will stop them…" to another 11B assigned to the HQ Platoon. We talked. He chain-smoked cigarettes as we stood out there guarding against an unseen threat. I don't recall anything we talked about. None of it made sense to me. We just stood there jabbering about nonsense. A short way behind the chain link fence separating Fort Myer from the rest of the world was the usually rather busy U.S. Highway 50, now resembling the traffic of an interstate in western Nebraska—that is, deserted. The shift ended and another couple guys from the platoon replaced us.

As lucky as I was to have an office to retreat to, I felt isolated from "my guys" in First Platoon. I walked down the command hallway to the First Sergeant's office to let him know.

"Genk," he said, "I understand what you're going through. I was injured once and put in a training detachment for a little while. Ended up missing out on the jump into Panama. I had a job to do, and so do you. Go do it well."

I noticed it was approaching midnight. We hadn't gotten any "word" on our role. I figured we would pull this security detail in the barracks for a few days before we were released to go home, but I was dead wrong. I opened my rucksack, took out my sleeping bag and pillow, put them on the floor and quickly fell asleep.

The next duty day arrived before I knew it. I don't recall much of that morning. There may have been a formation, as was standard for any duty day. I don't recall shaving or eating. This time is entirely lost to me. At some point that morning, the company's executive officer filled us in. We'd be conducting rescue and recovery operations inside the Pentagon beginning that night. Our company would be working the night shift. We were not to leave post (as if we could), get as much sleep as possible that day, and report at 1700 (could have been earlier, I don't really recall) with our Army-issued leather gloves with wool inserts and Kevlar helmets. I went back to my office, set my uniform for that evening aside, and laid back down, setting the alarm clock to 1600.

We regrouped that evening. After a "roll call" that was more of formality than anything else, we loaded up on the back of an LMTV and set off for our first night of work.

The HQ Platoon was assigned to do routine administrative tasks. We gathered accountability from the other three platoons every couple of hours, manned the radio, got supplies, etc. It was unbearably dull. I spoke to some of my buddies from First Platoon who'd been inside. They recalled the absolute destruction, the intense smell, and some body parts they'd found. I resolved to rejoin them on their next trip inside a couple hours later. I went to the XO and told him that I needed to be on the mission with my friends. They needed me and I needed to be with them. Without any hesitation, he agreed and told his fellow first lieutenant that I'd be joining the platoon for the duration of the operation.

I've repressed nearly all the memories I may have had from the rescue-and-recovery operation itself. I do recall being issued a protective mask that one might wear when they are applying paint to a wall. I recall shoveling debris from the ground into buckets as someone stood by to take the full bucket away. I think I remember being nearby when a guy found a hard hat with what we believed to be brain matter inside. I recall separating "personal effects" found near cubicles from official government documents. I remember seeing pieces of an American Airlines plane—large and small—scattered about several levels of the Pentagon, many corridors deep. I distinctly remember being very, very hot and sweaty with no relief. There were flood lamps all around, mostly to allow the firefighters sight of their Jenga-looking support structures. In short, it was miserable there, but intensely important. I remember thinking to myself, "No one could have survived this." I am not sure if anyone did. My memories of our time—those two weeks working inside the Pentagon after 9/11—are from the breaks in between shifts and back at the barracks for downtime. Even then, I don't recall eating or drinking anything. It is odd what one remembers from traumatic experiences like that….

With crystal clarity, I do remember the rides back to Fort Myer on the back of those LMTVs. I think we were all in shock on that first ride back as the hum of the tires on Washington Boulevard was the only sound, until one of the men let out, "Why do you build me up, Buttercup, baby, just to let me down? And mess me around…" We all joined in from there until the trucks came to a stop and we got down to the ground, seemingly forgetting what we'd all experienced the night before. The next two weeks are a blur. I know there was a tornado one night, but I don't recall much. I have a tough time separating what I witnessed with things I have seen on television or pictures posted on social media by other guys who were there. Sadly, I can't think of much else to say…

Our company would have the solemn duty of interring many of those who'd perished inside the Pentagon in Arlington National Cemetery over the following couple of weeks. I believe this provided some closure, at least in my life. I don't remember anything with any specificity, but I recall several tears streaming down my face while watching grieving family members who may not have had the chance to say goodbye to their fallen hero on the morning of September 11, 2001.

Earlier, I mentioned I had joined the Army for college money. That is true. I would re-enlist a few months later to extend my tour with the Old Guard. While the Army was at war in Afghanistan and Iraq, we buried the dead as they came through Dover. A few months after Operation Iraqi Freedom began, our company would be tapped to deploy to the Horn of Africa. I was very grateful to be a member of that team.

I would separate for a short while to take classes full time at George Mason University. One evening, I encountered an anti-war rally and got in the face of a kid who claimed that "9/11 was an inside job." I stated I had been there and witnessed unspeakable things, but among all the debris was most definitely parts of that airplane that flew into the side of the Pentagon. The kid was a true believer. He dismissed me as a useful idiot, part of the larger conspiracy. Dumbstruck, I left campus that day and re-enlisted in the Army Reserve. I would serve another six years and deploy twice more.

On the tenth anniversary of 9/11, several of the guys got together in Washington, D.C. We toured the barracks—which were in a sorry state—and went down to the 9/11 Memorial near Patton Circle in Arlington National Cemetery. I hope we have another reunion in 2021.

A Witness to Bravery

Andy Graff

I don't want to write this. There really isn't any better place to start. Much of what I will recount I have spent years putting behind me. Purposely forgetting, I think, on a subconscious level. Not from trauma, mind you; there are others who suffered far more than I, who witnessed worse, who carry burdens I cannot fathom. My emotions about my time in the Army revolve around feelings of inadequacy. Survivor's guilt, maybe. I don't know. I'm no psychologist. To assuage that guilt, I've let things go and moved forward. Now I've been asked to recount this experience and I feel the calling is noble. So here's my story.

I grew up in Utah. Yes, to answer the first question you have, in a Mormon family. My upbringing was excellent and my parents instilled in me the confidence to question the world and rationally apply logic and evidence to what I experience. To ask why and not settle for inadequate answers. This is a recurring theme for me and caused my parents distress as I came to the realization that god is pretend and religion is a refuge wherein people hide from the truth of their own mortality. Which I'm cool with. Love your religion. I just don't believe. Religion isn't for me. Yes, atheists join the military and love their country and want to fight to protect this divided and cracked and marvelous establishment that is the United States of America. This country that was founded by the religiously oppressed. Atheists aren't evil, folks, nor is religion the only path to ethics, morality, and decency. Get to know your friendly neighborhood atheist today!

For those of you still with me and not scandalized by my admission of atheism, here's the point: The biggest reason I chose to join the Army was to escape the overbearing religiosity that is Utah. I didn't want to be a missionary and try to convert people to a religion I don't believe, but I didn't know how to explain this to my family. So I chose a different way to serve. A path divergent from the one I had been brought up to expect. From the youngest age

I'd faced the notion that—as a Mormon—I would be "called to serve" a Mormon mission at the age of nineteen. It's what was expected. Demanded, even. To choose to not would result in scandal. To alleviate that scandal, I supplanted missionary with a different type of service. One I believed in. My choice. Five days after my seventeenth birthday my recruiting sergeant came by my house and I signed my name more times that I can count on more pages than I remember. Eleven months later, a week after graduation, I boarded a Delta flight from Salt Lake City to Denver to Atlanta.

In Denver I met another recent enlistee whom I'll call Jay. Jay and I spent our in-processing together at 30th AG and were pulled from the line at the same time by the Old Guard recruiter. In that recruiter's office we were asked if we'd like to be part of the Old Guard. We both said yes. He then told us that only one of us had ASVAB (that's the aptitude test for the military) scores high enough and the other would need a waiver. He asked us if the person with the low score should be given a chance and if we'd be willing to potentially give up our own chance. We both said the one with the waiver should get the opportunity, even if it meant we lost our own chance. He accepted us both and we went through basic training together in the same platoon and even ended up roommates in the Old Guard for a time.

I'm not going to focus too much on this, but it must be pointed out that, for the same reasons that led me to the Army and away from religion—namely, an inability to accept anything without extensive questioning and demands for explanation—I was a terrible soldier. I was often called "that guy" by my squad and platoonmates: When I witnessed an injustice (especially injustice to others) I'd complain, demand explanation, ask why, suggest a better way, rationally explain how my way was better, get in trouble, be yelled at, do a bunch of pushups, then have it done the way I suggested which was better for everyone, except I was on the shit list. I spent a lot of time on the shit list. It's what landed me as a member of the drafting team in Headquarters and Headquarters Company (HHC) and took me from Echo Company (called Honor Guard Company by Echo Company, but called Echo Company by everyone else). I'm fairly certain S-3 asked the First Sergeant for names of soldiers with security clearance and the First Sergeant's response was to send along his shit bird. That was me. The terrible soldier with a presidential security clearance. That clearance allowed me to work at the White House and near the president (I met presidents Clinton and Bush).

On 9/11 I woke and did the regular routine: smoke a bunch of cigarettes for breakfast then go do PT and run a bunch. I was nineteen, okay? Someone once told me they knew a runner who smoked a cigarette before running a marathon and it opened her lungs. So I ran with that as rationalization even though the science was anecdotal and horseshit. Fact was I was addicted and didn't want to quit. We all know smoking kills you. I quit a long time ago.

Stop judging, dammit. Quit smoking if you haven't. Or don't. Just know that shit does not open your lungs.

I was doughy-eyed that day. As an introvert (and a dork, if I'm honest), I'd always been terrified of girls. The previous weekend was Labor Day and I'd gone on a pass (or without a pass or any actual permission, I can't exactly remember, but the no pass version is most likely) to Massachusetts with a friend from Mass and met the most beautiful woman I'd ever seen in my entire life but she hooked up with my buddy and so I hooked up with her cousin instead and we even discussed trying to trade but I was too scared to broach that subject so I just went with it and now that was all I could think about because someone was interested in me and so I got twitterpated. Whew. The cousin ended up marrying another friend of mine and I got to marry that most beautiful woman who is also super smart and counterbalances my cynical pessimism by being one of the kindest people on the planet. That's another story, a continuing story, but it substantiates my mindset at the time. I had ladies on my mind and it was running nonstop at ninety and out of control from teenage hormones and infatuation. It was all I could think about.

After that morning's PT, I went into the S-3 area where I worked in the Old Guard headquarters building.

"Someone crashed their plane into the World Trade Center," said the captain of S-3 operations, bent over his computer screen. It was early and details had yet to emerge.

My mind was already whirring with imaginative futures and a gorgeous woman, so it picked right up on this information. In my mind was some idiot farmer in his crop-duster who was mad at the government or some bank or Danny DeVito and had flown his single-prop plane into a building, not causing much damage and really only killing himself. I remember something similar having happened a year or so earlier. In my imagination, the pilot had wild, curly hair and those old World War I–style goggles. I found it hilarious.

Yes. When I first heard a plane had crashed into the World Trade Center, I laughed. The pilot was just some dumbass. No big deal. He only hurt himself, right?

So, my team loaded into the S-3 van. It was a huge, maroon Dodge van. The full-size ones like the huge Mormon families had to buy to cart around their ten children back home. We didn't have any ceremonies to set up for that day and one of our team was leaving the Army. He needed help moving the junk out of his house at Fort Belvoir about twenty miles south of DC. We needed the van to move furniture. I hate moving furniture. I would have much rather spent the day moving furniture.

We were at Fort Belvoir when it all went to shit. A plane hit the Pentagon. That's a mile from Fort Myer. A mile from my bedroom. That's when I found out that it wasn't some dumbass in a prop-engine plane. That it wasn't an isolated incident.

A note on that bedroom. I was in the worst barracks building that existed on Fort Myer. It was shared among the Navy, Air Force, and the Army had the top floor. You couldn't drop a scrap of food on the floor or a war would break out between the mice and the ants to see who'd get it first. The mice lived in the air vents. Lots of them. We used to get drunk on the weekends and have competitions to see who could kill the most mice. I think the grand, all-time winner was twelve. Dude killed twelve mice in one night, and that's not even counting the other drunken participants.

Then there was the snake. Down another hall one of the soldiers kept two pythons as pets. They escaped. We found one quickly, but the other one was gone. For six months. Then a soldier came screaming down the hall. And there was the python. Larger, on the opposite side of the building, slithering back into the ventilation. We recaptured and re-caged it. Six months we'd figured it was dead, but it had been living on a smorgasbord of delicious mice. Six fucking months. I can only hope that building is long demolished. At least no one ever did room inspections or told us to clean up. And I didn't have to share a room, so it was a fair trade.

The first thing I did after being struck with the information of the Pentagon attack was call my mom. It took me a few tries to get through as the cell towers were overloaded, but if anyone needed to know that I was okay, anyone on the planet, she's that first call. I was calm.

We had the radio tuned to DC 101 at this point and no one knew what the fuck was going on. Conjecture poured across the airwaves. Planes were everywhere and on a collision course for the Capitol Building or the White House or their own house, according to callers. I remained calm. What else could I do? My only option at this point was to wait for orders. To trust that the system I had joined would function.

I heard our first set of orders. It wasn't a call to me, but to our team leader Chuck. It was through his cell phone and phones didn't have speakerphones then. But we all still heard it. Something along the lines of "Where the fuck are you? Get your fucking asses the fuck back here right the fuck now." And oh yeah, we didn't have permission to be at Fort Belvoir helping someone move with the government van that wasn't allowed to be used to help someone move. So, I didn't have to move much furniture that day. As I said, I wish moving furniture was the most that had happened.

The radio blared fear—the sky was falling and we were all doomed. We drove I-95 to I-395 and that's when I beheld a sight that is emblazoned in my memory: a giant black cloud of smoke pouring into the sky over a bridge spanning 395. It smeared its way across the sky. I grew up in Utah and I'm no stranger to wildfires. They happen every summer, especially around July 4

An image of the destruction, smoke, and frenzied activity shortly after the impact (photograph by Journalist First Class Mark D. Faram, USN).

when all of the idiots start blasting fireworks into dry desert fields. Clouds of smoke are familiar, but brush fire smoke is gray. This was an oil slick in the sky, crude and dark. I was already aware that the Pentagon had been struck, but it was this moment that it became understanding and realization. People were dead. Murdered.

Let's talk about that maroon government van. I would like you to imagine with me for a moment. Take a handful of adolescents—teenagers and an early twenty-something or two—and give them a big ass vehicle that they neither own nor care about. Let them drive that around. I'd wager there's some cringing going on about now.

It was required of us that our vehicles be combat parked. Every time. No exceptions. You had to back into the spot. No pulling in headfirst, even if you were in a rush and needed to dash inside and grab something you forgot. Back it in. Combat park. You're soldiers, dammit! The annoyance of this was compounded by the rule that anytime you backed up a vehicle, you needed a ground guide: someone outside the vehicle making sure you backed up safely and correctly. If someone took the van for a cleaning or to fill up with gas or to drop an NCO or officer off, it was required that a ground guide be used to combat park the vehicle. If I'm alone? I need to find another soldier, any soldier, to use as a ground guide. Or else. You didn't want to be the asshole caught pulling in headfirst; you especially didn't want to be the asshole caught backing up without a ground guide! A lot of the time I would wait for someone to be passing by on foot and just use them as a presumed ground guide. They'd let me know if I was about to hit them or run into a building or squish a dog, right? Right.

We also found another way around that. It was simple, really. Just drive the van like a humvee! Over the curb, across the sidewalk, over the three-inch concrete barrier, through the bushes, down the curb, and a rocking halt was the preferred way to park. And don't be the jackass who does it slowly. Hell no. You gun that engine and take the curb as hard as possible. And why not? It wasn't our van. It wasn't our money. Hell, funding for the military seems inexhaustible. They keep pouring in cash, so we'd burn that up with premium gasoline, what we called the "super ultra mega death wash" at the carwash (yes, that's exactly how I ordered the wash; "super ultra mega death wash, please"), and, of course, off-roading that van whenever the chance presented.

Today, however, we parked correctly. Did it by the book. Pulled in calmly and one of us got out as ground guide to back the van into its spot. There was a soldier outside in full combat regalia, one of the clerks from S-2, a private. Helmet, ALICE gear, M-16, rucksack. Yes, he was wearing his rucksack. I don't know why. Someone must have thought it was a good idea, but I'm still not even sure there was anything actually in the rucksack. I'm also not even sure he was issued any rounds for his rifle. Maybe he didn't have a rifle and my memory has failed me. Eyewitnesses are shit witnesses, after all. I'll never forget the look on his face, though. I'm sure it's the same look I had on my face the first time I couldn't get it up in bed (it happens to all of us, dammit!). Impotence. The world was burning and there wasn't a damn thing he could do about it. The best he had was putting on his rucksack and standing outside the headquarters building. He gazed across Summerall Field where generals retired to full Old Guard reviews, and across Arlington National Cemetery. He gazed at that plume of oil smoke that blackened the sky. He stared and impotence shone on his face. I could see his desire to sprint out there and help any way he could as it warred with his orders to stand there in a rucksack. And so he stood and stared.

We got chewed out, but it didn't last. There was shit to do. The Fort Myer fire department was down at the Pentagon already. Soon, it would be our turn. I was sent to deliver a message to the Echo Company CQ NCO to disseminate to the company or something like that. I can't exactly remember.

What I do remember is that I entered the Echo Company barracks, my original home as a soldier in the Old Guard.

"I don't give a fuck if I just worked twenty-four hours, First Sergeant," the CQ NCO from the previous day said. "I'm staying and I'm helping."

There were tears in the sergeant's eyes. He trembled. He was being sent home to rest, but he refused to leave. He'd just spent twenty-four hours straight at the CQ desk with no sleep or reprieve. He'd witnessed a terror attack from that post. The First Sergeant meant for him to go home and rest: after a twenty-four-hour CQ shift, you got the next day off. This sergeant refused. He was going nowhere. This was where he belonged and to hell with a day off. He would be part of the recovery effort, ordered or volunteer.

I'd never much liked the guy when we'd shared a platoon. He had been a specialist at the time and earned his promotion to sergeant after I left. Maybe I hadn't liked him much then, but I'd be damned if I didn't respect the hell out of him now. This is what he'd signed up for. To serve. To demonstrate courage in the face of hardship. He was a soldier and fuck it if he was going to go home and sleep when there was work to be done. What if there were people who needed his help? That's why he was there. Hell, that's why I was there.

We went to twelve-hour shifts. Twelve on, twelve off. As the planes over the U.S. were grounded, so were our ceremonies. The Old Guard pissed off the Virginia governor by heading up the Pentagon recovery instead of his national guard, but the Pentagon is an active duty installation and a place where we did a lot of our work. This was our calling and our job.

I worked as a driver and radio operator for the S-3 operations command. With my PSD security clearance, I was put in charge of making sure the radios were all encrypted. Washington, D.C., forgot its partisanship. We were all Americans together. As one. Outback Steakhouse and some other restaurants sent mobile kitchens to feed the soldiers involved in the recovery. Full Outback Steakhouse meals. Taco Bell gave us free food. We didn't have time to slow down and worry about food, so the DC community took care of us.

I never went into the Pentagon as part of the recovery. That wasn't my assignment. I'll admit to guilt about that, but I was just a PFC. It was my job to do as I was told and I was told to operate the radios, drive the major and sergeant-major, and keep the radio systems encrypted. I don't feel like I contributed what my fellow soldiers did, though. Rationally I know that I was a mechanism in a larger machine, that my actions were necessary, that I executed my function within the larger team; however, I feel like others were the ones who showed bravery, who stepped up as true soldiers.

There was the lieutenant I spoke with months later during our Expert Infantryman Badge training and evaluation. He was quiet while he told his story, as he looked out of the tent into the darkness of the trees at Fort A.P.

Hill. His hand shook as he mimed picking up a phone from the wreckage and looking at the screen. Of pressing a button and seeing the monochrome display show ninety-six missed calls.

There was another time when I drove the major over to the Pentagon and saw a quiet group of soldiers as they sat huddled together in their biohazard suits. They stared into the distance. Exhaustion wrapped their features. Others were nearby, just before or just after a shift. They ate meals from those many mobile kitchens that had set up. I'm not sure they tasted much.

There was the command NCO who lost her husband to the 9/11 attacks, another command NCO. A marriage of soldiers who had sacrificed for their country. Who sacrificed everything. A good friend and fellow soldier worked as her driver. She broke down when her dog died. The dog she had gotten with her late husband in lieu of children because they'd dedicated their lives to service. To protecting the citizens of the United States and the disparate beliefs and cultures and backgrounds that make up this country.

One former squad mate needed stitches and shots after his arm was sliced by debris. A young enlisted MP got a length of rebar through her leg. Claustrophobia struck others, depression, exhaustion. But that's what we were there for. That's why we became soldiers, to crawl through the shit and muck so that others don't have to. To protect those people we know and care about, and those we don't. To stand up for those whose beliefs are different, who vote for candidates we probably wouldn't, who worship in places and ways that are unfamiliar, who come to this country seeking the benefits and happiness and opportunities that are here, or are born to communities and regions that are different and feel odd. We didn't care about skin color or political affiliation or religious ideology. At the time, none of that mattered. Why it matters so much now, I don't know, but it makes me sad. Like we're rewinding.

While the 9/11 attacks were a pile of shit, it's undeniable that we came together as American citizens. As neighbors and colleagues. It affected us all.

Today I'm a teacher of English Language Arts. I found my propensity for instructing during my time as cadre for the Expert Infantryman Badge. I started my adulthood in service and it stayed with me. Now I serve the youth of our communities and it's the greatest job on the planet. I was never a hero. I did and have done nothing heroic. I know those who are, but I'm just a guy who wanted to help. I'm good with that. My time in the Army helped shape me into a person who fights his prejudices. I worked with soldiers from diverse backgrounds and cultures—cultures I never knew in the bubble of Mormonism that is Utah. And don't get me wrong. I like Mormons. I've raised my daughters in Utah, but Utah is its own interesting animal and my military experience provided me with a venue for exploring new ideas that I could never have encountered in Utah. I attended various church services for many different faiths. I met people from disparate places and experiences. One of the best soldiers that I knew was gay, though at that time it was something he had to hide (don't ask, don't tell) or risk being forced from the service. I watched women faster, stronger, smarter than me out-soldier the men around them. I saw the value of diversity, of opening my mind to the ideas and thoughts and feelings of other people. I met my wife. It made me a better person. It led me to be who I am today. Did I enjoy my time in the Army? Not really. If I had to go back to when I was seventeen, would I do it any differently? Would I choose another path? Might I eschew military service altogether? Not a chance.

Nights in White Coveralls

Jonathan Hoffman

I can only describe it as dreamlike. I follow a column of white-clad figures through a dark tunnel dramatically lit by work lights and headlamps. It's mostly dark in the daytime, too, sunlight barely reaching into the debris-filled cavern, so time is fluid and relative. I don't remember who is in front of me or behind; their faces are covered by 3M filtration masks, hardhats, and the hoods of paper-thin HazMat suits. Later, some of us decide to have our buddy write our last name on our back, or maybe that was dictated. We have been rotating through workers and people are constantly moving back and forth, up and down the single-file column.

Many of us have random tools in our hands: shovels mostly, or the odd sledgehammer. I recognize a few of my closer colleagues by their frame or eyes, men I have grown close with through such disparate environments as the steaming forests of Louisiana to chilly winter days working long hours in a cemetery. The place is as surreal as one can imagine. The chaotic and broken hulk of a modern-day office building. A winding path through mountains of corruption: fallen drywall, collapsed ceiling tiles, wiring, cabinets and furniture. And like a subterranean cave, water everywhere. The water flows between your legs, sometimes calf-deep, and trickles from the ceiling or down shredded concrete columns. It's gray when you shine your headlamp down, but we try not to do that. There are unknown obstacles hidden in the water, so you have to drag your boots along in order to not trip. And the smell. In subsequent years, I would come to understand how immediately a smell can bring flashbacks to mind. Innocently, a waft of perfume may remind you of your long-passed aunt. The thick haze of an approaching thunderstorm can bring nostalgia of a long-ago Ohio summer afternoon, riding bikes to the end of the earth with your best friend. But in the years following 9/11, I

Recovery personnel continue their efforts through the evening and into the early morning hours (photograph by CPL Jason Ingersoll, USMC).

would be reminded through that smell—by campfires, by burning trash pits in Afghanistan, by simply soldering wiring together on my truck—of these nights. It is not anything like the smell of death, but rather of all the things one would find in normal daily life suddenly burned and disintegrating. Not the pleasant wood smoke of an autumn campout; rather, if someone used that fire to burn plastic and melt metal. So even as I write this nearly 18 years later, I can clearly match that smell with this dark place.

As a sheltered kid raised in the conservative heartland of the U.S., I'd had only fantasies of honor and glory in mind when I enlisted in 1996. I grew up during the 1980s near Wright Patterson Air Force Base (WPAFB), memorizing every aircraft that flew overhead—constant reminders of the Soviet boogeyman that in a few short years would all but disappear. I spent entire summers with neighborhood friends in the nearby woods. Fewer than maybe a hundred acres, but for us it might as well have been the Yukon. Early on, we would play soldiers, throwing pinecone grenades at make-believe Commies or debating which stick resembled an M16.

I was active in Boy Scouts even before I could join. I idolized my three older brothers (we would ultimately all earn our Eagle—still a point of pride for our mother) and was adopted by the local Troop at our church as their "mascot." I quickly became very eager due to the patriotism espoused by

Scouting, and while our adult leaders (many of whom were Vietnam veterans) tried to downplay any connection with militaristic ideals, some of us boys drew strong parallels with the military "culture." By "culture," I essentially mean movies. I had seen nearly every war movie made up to that point and saw nothing greater than to do my part in fighting in what my teenage brain thought was a clear battle of good vs. evil. Even the very clear anti-war motifs of films like *Apocalypse Now* and *Platoon* were lost on me. Decades before I had heard of confirmation bias, I fell in love with the honor and romance of war and cast aside any depictions of its horrors and stupidity. By 17, I was an Army recruiter's ideal shoo-in, and very, *very* naïve.

My dad was a child of the 1940s and '50s and knew only of the post-war and God-given might and Manifest Destiny of the United States—the original *America First* mentality. He had served in the U.S. Air Force in the 1960s, in the precursor of what would come to be known as Signals Intelligence. He fortunately never went to Vietnam, but instead, with my mom, raised a family of four boys and a girl. Through 8mm reels, he painstakingly documented our youths through the 1970s and '80s in the suburbs of Dayton, Ohio. My dad was not easy to grow up with; his generous and loving goodwill clashing with his narrow-minded and strict adherence to conformity, and above all, following the word of God. He continued to work at WPAFB in the Foreign Technology Division, now known as the National Air and Space Intelligence Center, until he retired in the mid–90s.

My mom's story is one of local legend and, to anyone who knows her, she is less a diminutive woman than a force of nature. Born like my dad in 1939, her birth home was in Pomerania, now western Poland. She came into the world literally as the *Panzerkampfwagen* rolled eastward, igniting the Second World War. Her father, though an older family man, was conscripted late in the war and sent to the front. No word ever returned as to his fate.

In early 1945, she and her brothers and sister, their mother leading with a third baby boy at her breast, would narrowly escape through the harsh winter. A month-long trek by foot to the port of Danzig (now Gdansk) would see her infant brother die—her mother was too starved to produce milk. The oldest sister, Krystal (16) would save her mother and remaining younger siblings by scrounging for scraps and abandoned crops or begging at the few not-yet-abandoned churches. The family barely made it to the Baltic in time to be evacuated as part of Operation Hannibal. As they departed the harbor, the children would witness the torpedoing of other ships carrying both civilians, casualties, and troops. The latter passengers, along with possible anti-aircraft artillery (this is debated), made these fleeing vessels legitimate military targets for the Soviet dive-bombers and artillery. The family made it safely to Denmark, where they stayed several months in a Danish refugee camp through the end of the war. They would resettle in the central German state of Thuringia and the oldest sister, my Aunt Krystal, would emigrate to Cincinnati, Ohio. She raised money as a nanny and sponsored my mom to work as an au pair for a wealthy Jewish family. My mom came to the U.S. in 1954.

My parents would meet and marry in 1962, as my dad was a senior in the Air Force ROTC at Asbury College near Cincinnati. My mom was by then finishing Nursing School and would off-and-on work as a nurse for the next 40 years.

By 1996, I was essentially done with life in suburban Ohio, and couldn't wait to leave. I was not a good student throughout high school and while I now recognize most kids that age are glaringly socially awkward, I felt increasingly ostracized. My few friends were active in bands and, increasingly, drugs. While my test scores were sometimes above average, my homework was no match for girls, pot, and part-time jobs. By senior year, I had dropped most of my classes. I knew I had no chance in pursuing more and harder education that I would have also have to find a way to pay for.

I walked into the recruiter's office with a friend of mine, who was maybe interested in enlisting as a mechanic or other trade. Once the rotund Staff Sergeant put the laser disc in, my doubts were losing against the sense that between my Boy Scout experiences and years of glorifying this culture, I had no other real direction *except* to join up. My dad tried to convince me to choose a trade skill: engineering, mechanic, computers. Anything but "cannon fodder." My mom, of course, wept, which I took simply as her not wanting her baby to grow up. Later I would realize that it was from her own experiences, witnessing what war was and knowing firsthand what soldiers could be exposed to, the horrors they might take part in.

My adolescent machismo told me that if I was to be a soldier, it would have to be whatever the best was. So, the recruiter convinced me to sign-up for the Airborne Infantry, and in June '96 I was off.

My first duty assignment, Fort Campbell, Kentucky, sits on the Tennessee and Kentucky border and is home to the famed 101st Airborne Division. With this unit I spent nearly four years in a state of almost nonstop training, deploying to training centers around the U.S., and for six months on a peacekeeping rotation in Egypt.

Early on in our relationship, my first wife (we met and married in 1998) began showing symptoms of rather mysterious and seemingly unrelated medical conditions. By 2000, when my first enlistment was set to end and we had two children and no degrees or career prospects, we decided to seek a change of station to Washington, D.C. The Army occasionally can "compassionately reassign" soldiers whose family members have complicated medical problems. So, in the summer of 2000, we loaded up our little family—a six-year-son and one-year-old baby girl—into a U-Haul and drove to our new life in Washington.

Like most people who have never served in the 3rd U.S. Infantry, I had no idea what to expect from such a different unit. I had been often told that the application process was very rigid, and indeed I was required to resubmit my application a couple of times due to my security clearance and other factors. I knew from my experience in Basic Training that a few soldiers were selected as recruits to go to the Old Guard (affectionately known in-house as TOG)—every unit needs Privates, after all. But when I arrived, I was surprised (to say the least) that the vast majority of the regiment's soldiers and junior NCOs were serving on their first assignment. I can remember only perhaps two other soldiers under the rank of Sergeant who had come from elsewhere in the Army. Ostensibly, this was of no concern at all. It was immediately apparent that my new peers and NCOs were incredibly disciplined when it came to the main, ceremonial mission of the regiment, even if untrained in normal Infantry tactics.

Garrisoned on Fort Myer (now known as Joint Base Myer–Henderson Hall), Virginia, the unit is housed in the center of Arlington. The eponymous cemetery (ANC) is roughly shaped like a 600-acre circle in between Arlington and Alexandria and bordering the Potomac River across from the capital. Fort Myer sits like a crescent alongside the western edge of the cemetery, with direct access for funeral and ceremony traffic and for guards of the famous Tomb of the Unknowns, located in its midst.

The Old Guard's mission in the summer of 2000 centered almost entirely on ceremonies in and around the Military District of Washington (MDW), with each of its five infantry companies rotating between assigned weekly tasks. "Primary" Week meant that company was entirely focused on executing funerals. The "Backup" company provided support for any funerals that could not be accomplished by the Primary unit, as well as any other ceremonies that were required. These would range from senior Army retirements to arrivals of foreign heads of state, to the cemetery or the Pentagon. Finally, the "Detail" company(ies) would be given any ancillary tasks or use the time for field training (bear in mind that this was still, in name at least, an infantry regiment). A subtask to this latter training was called Civil Disturbance Operations. We kept on hand a supply of Riot Control gear (batons, plexiglass body and face shields, etc.) in the event of emergencies in Washington, such as the IMF and World Bank Protests in the Spring of 2000. During these rotations, we would have equipment readiness drills and emergency notification exercises to test our reaction time, and passes/leaves were minimized in case the company on the "CD Ops" cycle was needed in an emergency. Our field training mostly came once per year in the form of perhaps a week-long exercise at Fort AP Hill, near Fredericksburg, where we would focus on purely the most fundamental combat tactics.

Each of the "line companies"—that is, Bravo, Charlie, and Delta—were organized into three Platoons. The 1st Platoon (Escort) was the marching platoon, largely tasked with marching for the more complex, Full Honors funerals. The 2nd Platoon (Caskets) performed as pallbearers and folded the flag from the coffin to give to the family of the deceased. And the 3rd Platoon (Firing Party) provided the seven riflemen and their commander for the twenty-one-gun salute. I was placed into the 2nd Platoon of Bravo Company, or *Battlehard*, likely because I was of a larger frame (I had never been thin), and most of the bigger men were wanted as casket bearers. I fell in quickly with my squad, making several friends that I bonded with through long days in the cemetery, often completing six funerals each day in the heat, rain, and snow of the Mid-Atlantic. When not performing funerals, we would spend much time practicing. Folding the flag, in particular, is an extremely intricate maneuver requiring each of the six (for standard honors) or eight (for full honors) soldiers to perfectly meet his marks to the proper cadence. The soldier is expected to move almost robotically, never breaking what is known as *ceremonial composure*, or making any extra shuffles or even a casual turn of the head. Because of the nature of the work and how the platoon is split into three squads, there is obviously a healthy rivalry between the teams for who would be perceived as best. The Regimental HQ also ran a certification system by which each team would be graded on a real funeral in the cemetery every quarter. So, every day during primary and often during the other weeks, it was not uncommon to see casket teams, or firing parties, or marching elements practicing their specific tasks in and around the company areas. It was even possible to drive by Fort Myer on U.S. Route 50 and hear the three volleys of the firing party as they practiced behind the barracks.

Time went quickly working at the brutal pace of the Old Guard. It was very different from the 101st, where most days were taken up by training in the field or preparing to train in the field. During the summer, the mission could be so draining that often we would not dare to perform physical training in the morning for fear of soldiers "falling out" of a ceremony due to heat exhaustion or fatigue. Living 20 miles south of Washington in Fort Belvoir, I often would not walk in the door before 7 p.m., after a 60- to 75-minute commute and 12-hour day. I was quickly forced to admit that though the tempo of this new assignment was different from that of a regular Army unit, and nearly every night I could expect to be home with my family, it was far tougher than I had given it credit. Days and weeks blended together through the Winter. I was promoted to Sergeant in Spring of 2001. The Army decided to make us wear berets on that June 14 (the Army's birthday), much to the chagrin of nearly every soldier I knew.

The Old Guard performed a large event labeled Spirit of America (SOA) nearly every year, in the early 2000s, at least. This was a large event executed in the huge MCI (now Verizon) Center in downtown Washington. It included

Army marching bands, marching elements of the Old Guard, and soldiers dressed as their predecessors from throughout American history and acting out live-action scenes on the arena floor. Because I had served in the 101st Airborne, I happened to be qualified to rappel along with several other soldiers. So one of my parts in this show, along with perhaps seven or eight other NCOs, was to drop from the catwalk of the arena some 110 feet above the surface. Looking back, I recognize it more as what it obviously was: a huge public relations and recruiting effort by the Army in a time when new joins had been plummeting, correlating with the economic highs of the late '90s.

The 2001 Spirit of America program was scheduled for the latter part of September. My friends in Bravo Company and I were excited that the end of the chaotic and grueling summer was upon us. The cooling temperatures of the coming autumn were always welcomed as a sign that the "battle rhythm" would ease substantially. Those of us who were given specific parts in the show were allowed extra time for preparation, and the remainder of the company spent the days of that early and peaceful September conducting Civil Disturbance training and preparing for the upcoming cycle of "CD Ops."

So it was mostly a routine morning on that Tuesday in September. It was clear and refreshingly cool after wearing a wool uniform through the blazing heat of the Virginia summer. The group of us designated to rappel at the upcoming show were scheduled to be in the large marching hall down the street from our barracks at 9 a.m. As I walked down the stairs of the barracks to head to the training, my acting supervisor approached me and said, "Some idiot flew a plane into the World Trade Center," punctuated by spits of Copenhagen. Thinking it was something like a single-engine Cessna, I made my way to the dayroom, only to be confronted with dozens of men from the company glued to the huge Sony. I was in my rappelling gear and maybe this reminded me that others would likely be waiting on me, so I left to join my fellow NCOs and our belayers at the marching hall.

Arriving there, I found that the soldier who was meant to belay me was not present and I ran back to the company to speed him along. I found him with the rest of the unit watching as now both towers burned, a sight which made me forget his tardiness. I always felt lucky that I didn't see in real time as Flight 175 hit the South WTC Tower.

The unit was rallied to the quad in between the barracks, where, perhaps an hour later, our First Sergeant (1SG) told us that "Some jackass decided to fly a jet into the Pentagon," approximately a mile away from where we stood. We were told to stand by, and a hundred men commenced babbling like schoolgirls.

Things from this point have become somewhat hazy through the intervening years. I called my wife and told her I was okay, but that I wouldn't be home anytime soon. I tried to call my parents but would only find out later that they were spending the week at their long-time getaway resort near Indiana. My older brother heard the voicemail and tracked them down through the park rangers the next day. They hadn't heard anything of the news from their campsite.

We had our gear prepared for an emergency deployment, if needed, and the company was presumably prepared for contingencies based on our duty rotation. But we stayed that night at our barracks. There was rampant conjecture as young soldiers and seasoned veteran NCOs talked nervously and excitedly about just what the hell had happened and what they would do with us. There was even speculation coming from higher that we would be deployed into the Capital with live ammunition to safeguard vital buildings or terrain. Such was the chaotic and wondering environment that first evening. Traffic throughout the region was blocked and cellphone lines were completely down. We would learn later that one of our sister companies (I believe it was Delta) had been performing a funeral only a few hundred yards from where the airplane impacted the Pentagon.

The second evening after, we were loaded onto LMTV trucks (the more modern "deuce and a half") with some light equipment. As we rode in the canvas-covered back, past the Iwo Jima Memorial and down Route 110, it was our first breath of a new world that no one among us would really comprehend yet. Cars pulled onto the breakdown lane to let us pass. Drivers honked and passengers cheered and waved and snapped photos. A lifted pickup carried two large American flags flying from the tailgate and kids in the bed stared in awe at the first soldiers in combat gear they had likely ever seen. I think it was that image in my head that made me realize how quickly the world had changed and how just that weekend, only three days before, seemed so innocent and carefree and far away. Further down, civilian traffic was diverted, and we caught our first glimpse of the ravaged building. It's a hard thing to describe in retrospect, so I'm thankful that pictures of the site are readily found. We walked across the now-closed lanes of Route 27, to the staging area. What until 24 hours before had been a grassy field and helipad was covered with myriad emergency vehicles, construction equipment, tents, debris, and hundreds of people. Uniforms and lettered vests of every law enforcement and government agency one could imagine milled through the scene, the building hulking in the background with the large and angry gash. There was no sign of an airplane and looking at the scene one could hardly believe that somewhere in there was a passenger jet full of *people*.

The first night at the scene, we were assigned to a large tent (I don't remember if we erected the tent or not) adjacent but perhaps 100 meters from the northwest side that we saw almost daily from Section 64 of the cemetery. The platoons were given work shifts spread throughout three different locations on the site. Working in the building itself was soon called "Recovery," but some members of the company decided on the more unfortunate moniker of "Bag and Drag." At the time, this seemed to me as very callous and plain awful, but then who can blame young men barely out of high school for how they respond to something so grisly?

The second objective was guarding the perimeter of the north parking lot of the Pentagon, on the far side of the building towards the Potomac. This was where the FBI would attempt to recreate the entire Boeing 757 as it was taken piece by piece from the building. Of arguably even more importance, this was where all human remains from the site would be taken. Soldiers from the Puerto Rican National Guard would soon arrive, mortuary affairs specialists who would assist the FBI in recovering and identifying as many victims as possible.

The third section that was to be worked was inside of the building itself, where teams of our soldiers secured the interior access to the damaged side of the structure. After all, the surviving 25,000 employees of the Department of Defense would still have to operate their headquarters.

The most physically and emotionally demanding duty was, of course, the Recovery work. The first night we went in, the only protective gear we wore was a thin carpentry-style mask, our issued Kevlar helmets, and latex gloves under our leather work gloves. Many of us wore jungle-style boots, often preferred for their light weight and breathability. The latter attribute not a great thing when standing and walking all night in gray, ankle-deep water. Later, perhaps even by the second night, we had been issued the lightweight white suits, hardhats and 3M filtration masks that can be seen in many photographs.

The main chasm carved by the impacting aircraft created instability all around that area. Therefore, firefighters and engineers had chosen an entrance approximately 100 meters to the north—or left—of the crater. To mark this entrance, a standard size American flag was hung by the hole. The tactic was simple. The laboring soldiers, a flexible source of manpower, would follow a small team of firefighters and engineers. The latter specialists would identify where debris could be safely removed from, and then quickly build a column of large, 8 × 8 inch lumber, like a kids Lincoln Log cabin, in order to shore up the ceiling. Then the area around this column could safely be cleared wider by the soldiers and other workers. The path wound through the ground floor like a snake, necessary because of the higher floors' instability. This was where our soldiers were the most benefit, speeding the progress by carrying large pieces in teams, armloads of debris, and shovelfuls of muck to the exterior of the building. All in an effort to reach the aircraft, and most importantly the flight recorder, as rapidly as was safe. These shifts coalesce in memory. On perhaps our second night of this work, after we had received our protective equipment, we began seeing more and more pieces of the destroyed jetliner. In one instance, a group of perhaps six of us was asked to remove one of the large jet fans, weighing perhaps a couple of hundred pounds, through the twisting pathway. This was particularly noteworthy at the time, as it bore such a strange and macabre relation to how we carried caskets in the cemetery only just recently.

Many stories were passed around our small unit of what particular and grisly horrors individuals had witnessed in the midst of the destruction. Someone would lament seeing a nearly preserved office, surrounded by the burnt and broken cavity. Preserved that is, except for the charred remains of a man at his desk, one arm fixed uselessly as a shield against the coming blast that killed him. Another entire squad, I believe from 3rd Platoon, was overheard excitedly jabbering about how gruesome their particular shift had been. One singularly awful sight received the name from some of the younger soldiers of the "man in the machine." In one instance, one of my friends (I can't remember who) I was working closely with that first night to clear debris from the ground was using a sort of snow-shovel, pushing it through the water. I believe I was there holding the flashlight and taking turns. Each shovelful was thrown into a wheelbarrow under the careful watch of an FBI agent. The agent was there to identify any possible evidence or human remains. In one load, I spotted something shiny and reached out, not seeing the tuft of long blond hair. The agent quickly grabbed the fragment of the woman's face and gently placed it into the red biological waste bag he carried. We knew at the time, of course, that giving such testimony and monikers to these nightmares was perhaps improper, or, at the very least, indecent. However, at the same time, in the chaotic and unspeakable environment that we were working in, maybe some of us quickly forgave ourselves. We were dealing with horrors that most of us, at the average age of perhaps 22 years, certainly had never dealt with. In the subsequent 18 years of wars, many of us would go on to see even worse atrocities against human beings, some of these even at our own hands. So, in hindsight, I do forgive my younger self and my peers for our reactions to these things, which often bordered on dark humor or at the very least excited gossip.

Certainly plenty of books and papers have been written about the horrors of war versus violence in our own country, especially after 11 September 2001. Maybe it was that what we were witnessing in the Pentagon was so near our home, and our daily job, our commuter routes and grocery stores, and this added to the surreal and insane nature.

As the days and nights wore on, the flight recorder was discovered and more and more area was cleared, ultimately by small bulldozers after the structure was sufficiently reinforced. We would move to higher floors. On one exhausting night shift, our platoon was asked to move several dozen huge safes and filing cabinets, tossing them unceremoniously out of the second or third floor windows and onto the piles of rubble below. Some of us wondered what secrets were locked away inside those waterlogged and impossibly heavy pieces. Often, we would find hundreds of personal effects, especially as the offices further away from the point of impact saw less damage but still needed clearing. Thousands of pictures, framed degrees and awards, souvenir mugs, children's' artwork. One cabinet contained thousands of blank military "challenge" coins, the sort soldiers often carry in their pockets or display on a desk. We spent our lunch break, in between bites of MREs, skipping these across the derelict rings of the building to break the windows on the other side. These things in retrospect sound so unprofessional, of course, but at the time seemed like an opportunity to blow off stress in a most casual way.

Not every night of our work was spent in such grisly fashion, as when we worked on the recovery detail. A few nights we guarded the North Parking Lot, where the large 757 was being painstakingly recreated piece by piece as the wreckage was recovered from the building. This was, after all, a very large and dynamic crime scene that the FBI was frantically trying to figure out. Though most of the civilian traffic had been diverted from this area, the occasional bystander was able to drive by and attempt to video tape what little they could see through the hastily constructed security fence. A number of times, our soldiers and NCOs asked passersby to stop filming, and perhaps some of these items were even confiscated.

The third detail we were asked to work was the interior security of the building. This was seen by many of us as the most redundant and—gratefully—mundane duty on the site. Looking back now after many years of leading and tasking soldiers, I think this guard duty was an intentionally dull job given by our superiors as a break from the physically and mentally exhausting recovery duty while still keeping us nearby in case of other requirements. There were, of course, still organic Pentagon security forces on site, as well as firmly secured doors preventing anyone from accessing the damaged portions of the building. So, these nights were mostly spent by us doing what soldiers do best—namely bullshitting and goofing off.

Around the site of the recovery effort, a small army of support personnel had arrived over the first few days. This swelled to hundreds by the end of the first week, and this collection of charities, NGOs, and official government functions was named Camp Unity. Here one could find every sort of assistance, from the USO offering food, the Red Cross giving massages, and Army Chaplains and psychologists offering much-needed perspective on the insane experiences people were working through. We felt almost guilty by the outpouring of so much sincere support, and many of us likely became lifelong supporters of the charities whose volunteers spent as many hours as we did at the recovery site.

I cannot recall if we were released to go home after the first night on the ground at the Pentagon, or if it was the second night. But I do remember that first morning, perhaps 8:00, driving south on I-95 towards Fort Belvoir. I remember because I was overwhelmed and weary and probably should not have been driving. The traffic was unusually light, and I pulled over onto the breakdown lane as I listened to a song on the radio. It was the first time I had heard Five for Fighting's *Superman (It's Not Easy)*, and I laid my head on the steering wheel and fell apart, sobbing from exhaustion. I was at a loss of what I would say to my wife and our children. I felt like everything in life, even my ability to keep my family safe, had changed. When I got home, I peeled off my filthy, camouflage BDUs, placed them in a trash bag, and asked my wife—against her protests—to throw it in the dumpster.

The later days working at the site became more routine, Donald Rumsfeld and President Bush visited at some point. We were added back into the flow of performing funerals. We buried victims of the attack in Arlington—for many of us the first funerals of active duty soldiers that we had taken part in. Of particular note was that of LTG Timothy Maude, the highest-ranking American officer to die by foreign action since 1945. The final day we spent at the Pentagon site was 1 October, when the actual mission changed from one of recovering aircraft parts and human remains to an anti-terror investigation. Soldiers from our platoon received the American flag from the doorway that hundreds of firefighters, construction engineers, agents and soldiers had used for weeks and folded it in the same style as an interment flag. In a small ceremony, in front of the large gash carved in the building, one of our squad mates presented the flag to Robert Mueller, then the FBI Director.

The next couple of years at the Old Guard were a testament to how drastically things had changed for our unit and the country. Days after the attacks brought fears of anthrax, as five people died after receiving the toxin in the mail. Within only a few weeks we would witness the interment of Johnny "Mike" Spann, a CIA covert operative and the first American killed in the American invasion of Afghanistan. Our security mission, that we had largely joked about before as being redundant and unnecessary, now was a large part of our job. We placed teams of soldiers on the gates, augmenting the organic security forces, in an effort that would come to be called Operation Noble Eagle and is actually still in progress throughout the United States. This sidemission continued through the following year and was a large part of our job outside of the ever-present funerals that remained the priority for the Old Guard.

With the beginning of the Iraq War in 2003, and the accelerating conflict in Afghanistan, the Army found itself stretched thin of infantry units to deploy, especially to the myriad smaller requirements around the globe. In late 2003, our company was deployed to the tiny East African nation of Djibouti.

There we spent nine months training some of the regional military forces in modern tactics and acting as security teams for various civil affairs efforts in Djibouti, Ethiopia, and Kenya.

Returning to Virginia in 2004, I stayed on with Bravo Company for four more years and ultimately served as the chief of the "Colors" Squad, responsible for leading all color guard missions and supervising much of the unit's marching training and ancillary ceremonies. I was approached in 2008, as I was preparing to leave, with a once in a lifetime offer to work with the U.S. Congress as a travel and escort NCO. So, for the next two years, I traveled the globe on dozens of Congressional Delegations with members and leaders of the House and Senate.

Deciding it was finally time to leave the Beltway, my next destination would be Baumholder, Germany, then home to the 170th Infantry Brigade. Having served in Washington in a ceremonial organization for over half my career, I was deeply anxious about returning to the regular force, especially with the knowledge that these units had been deploying over and over for nearly a decade. I completely expected to deploy almost immediately upon reassignment, and so I spent months trying to update myself on what might have changed in the "line infantry" as well as the military's latest efforts in counterinsurgency, or COIN. Considering Barack Obama's win and his campaign promise of leaving Iraq, matched with the renewed increase of forces back to Afghanistan, I felt sure that we would be sent there. The first year of my assignment in Germany was near constant training, but a few weekends my family and I were lucky enough to enjoy Western Europe. Perhaps my mom's heritage helped spurn it along, but I very quickly fell in love with living in Germany and mused that perhaps someday I would be able to live there after my service had ended.

My company was chosen in May of 2010 to participate in the Russian VE Day parade, an unprecedented invitation by Putin that has not been repeated. We were honored to march in Red Square on the 65th anniversary of the Allied Victory, alongside nearly 100,000 Russian, former Soviet Socialist Republic, British, and French troops. This remains one of the highlights of my career, as one of fewer than 100 American infantry soldiers to ever march with bayonets fixed in front of the Kremlin.

Our deployment in 2011 to the north of Afghanistan was, by providence, largely unremarkable. Before the deployment my commander had learned of my interests in foreign policy and my research in COIN. I had thought that I was just catching up to my peers after so many years of "sandbagging" in Washington, but to my surprise found that the tenants of counterinsurgency were largely new to most soldiers at the tactical level. So, for half of the deployment, while our unit's main effort was development projects and training, I served as the lead trainer and governance adviser. Mostly I worked with the command, USAID and its German equivalent GIZ, and the local Afghan government in Kunduz to prioritize and fund civil infrastructure projects. These local and regional development initiatives were one of the cornerstones of the COIN strategy—theoretically, if you improve life for the people and stabilize their lives, the incentives to join the Taliban should diminish. The second half of the deployment, I served as a squad leader. We completed dozens of patrols both on foot and in our 20-ton MRAPs, in and around the Kunduz province and finished the year-long mission by training the regional police and militia in counterterrorism fundamentals.

Unfortunately, the Army would not let us stay in Europe any longer and we were next sent to Fort Benning, Georgia. This large base is where all infantry soldiers begin their lives in the Army and is also home to some of the toughest military training, including Ranger School. I was not excited to be back there, especially in the middle of the South, where I had always felt uncomfortable. However, by serendipity, I was to find myself in the best job of my career—training new infantry Lieutenants. The Infantry Basic Officer Leader Course is a four-month school for newly commissioned, future platoon leaders. As the first real military training many of these young people received outside of ROTC or West Point, the course takes them from practically being a civilian to a trained leader who can potentially take a 40-soldier platoon to combat. Having always loved training soldiers, but with not much patience for the often-low motivation (or comprehension, for that matter) of privates, I found this to be a very rewarding experience. Recognizing the human capital raised by even one cycle of the school, say 120–150 lieutenants, through quality and effective training in all soldier skills from marksmanship and land navigation to more advanced platoon maneuvers and tactics, I felt that this was truly the culmination of my career.

My Old Guard

Fines E. Kiper II

For as long as I can remember, my father spoke about the military and law enforcement. I wanted to serve in the military and be a federal agent from junior high on up. I remember dressing up in Army fatigues and playing soldier as a kid. When you are a third-generation law enforcement officer, serving others tends to run in the blood. My grandfather and father served in both the U.S. Army and in law enforcement. My grandfather, after whom I'm named, was a member of the greatest generation. He served in the 82nd Airborne Division in the 405th Infantry Regiment. The Nazis referred to this unit as "Devils in Baggy Pants," because of the type of pants the soldiers wore. My father was a police officer for 33 years, working at the municipal, county, and state levels. Both men played a significant role in my life, even though I never met my grandfather. He died well before I was "a glint in your daddy's eye," as my father would say. My father used to tell me stories of him and it was almost mythical how my grandfather was portrayed. Needless to say, I was inspired by each one's service in the military and law enforcement.

When you grow up in a small town—Artesia, New Mexico, to be exact—you can't wait to leave. I couldn't wait to live in a big city, out on my own, as a federal agent. I wanted to follow in the footsteps of my father and grandfather before him. Everything I did throughout high school and college was preparation for my own military and law enforcement career. I played sports, attended my father's alma-mater, New Mexico Military Institute (NMMI), studied criminal justice and government courses, and achieved the rank of Cadet Captain. Prior to NMMI, I attended the U.S. Army Basic Camp in Fort Knox, Kentucky, for a six-week program for Reserve Officer Training Corps (ROTC). I decided not to pursue Army ROTC at that time because I had my heart set on the Navy. While at NMMI, I applied for the Naval Academy. I wanted to become a Naval officer and be assigned to an aircraft carrier. My appointment to the Naval Academy did not materialize like I had hoped.

Upon graduation from NMMI, I enrolled and transferred to Texas Tech University, where again I studied courses in sociology and political science, concentrating my electives in criminal justice. During my senior year at Tech, I began pursuing the Navy Officer Candidate School (OCS). During this time, I learned they were offering recruits a student loan repayment option if they joined as an enlisted soldier. I ultimately decided this was the most feasible way to pay off my student debt that I had incurred while attending Tech. It wasn't the Navy and it wasn't as an officer, but I thought to myself that this is what I was more familiar with since I had attended the Basic Camp for Army ROTC, as well as attended NMMI. I entered the Delayed Entry Program (DEP) in November 1998, with a basic training date of August 12, 1999, my birthday.

Nothing like telling your family goodbye to start a whole new way of life. I can still see the view from my airplane window seat looking at my dad and my sister, along with her family, as they were watching from the terminal window as my airplane departed for the runway in Albuquerque.

When I enlisted in the Army, I chose the 82nd Airborne Division as my station of choice. I was going to serve in an infantry division and jump out of airplanes like my grandfather. I kept pushing the option to become an officer down the road, knowing it would always be there. Becoming an officer in the military had always been one of the goals of service. At the time of my DEP enlistment, Airborne School was not included in my contract. I was assured by my recruiter that upon my arrival to Fort Bragg, North Carolina (home of the 82nd Airborne Division) for my initial duty assignment and station of choice that it would be included in my enlistment contract and I would then be sent to Airborne School. This was somewhat of a loophole for enlistment contracts.

Things changed on August 12, 1999, when I arrived at the Military Entrance Processing Station or MEPS. I was met by another recruiter who informed me that I could not be assigned to an airborne unit if I did not have Airborne School in my enlistment contract. There had been a policy change the Army implemented to close this loophole. At the time, I remember asking where I would be assigned. The recruiter said he would make my Military Occupational Series (MOS) as 11X or Infantry Undecided. Your MOS designates what job you will perform in the Army. Originally, I was an 11B, your standard infantryman; so, as an 11X, that meant I had no idea where I was going to be stationed. This policy change impacted my station of choice, played a crucial role in my decision to join the Old Guard, and ultimately impacted my career in the Army. After arriving to Fort Benning, GA, where Infantry Basic Training was held, we were assigned to the 30th AG Reception Battalion, the processing unit for new recruits.

During my time at the reception battalion, I was introduced to the Old

Guard. One evening after dinner, we were told to line up in two lines facing each other. An E-5 Sergeant from the Old Guard announced to everyone that as he walked by you and told you to "Go," you were to immediately step out of line and return to the barracks. He walked up and down the line doing as he said, telling recruits to either "Stay" or "Go." Fortunately, I was told to stay. Looking back now, some 20 years later, all I can say is I was extremely lucky and sometimes wonder why the recruiter had chosen me. Once the recruiter had finished walking down both lines, he gathered everyone in and explained what and who the Old Guard was. I was almost immediately sold. I knew where I would be stationed, and I knew the Honor Guard was a unique assignment. The Old Guard was stationed at Fort Myer, Virginia, across the Potomac River from Washington, D.C. During the summer of 1998, I applied and became an intern for Senator Pete Domenici of New Mexico. I spent six weeks living in the George Washington University dorms and riding the D.C. Metro train to Union Station and walking to the Russell Senate Office Building for work. Every weekend I was out seeing the museums, the monuments, and the rest of what the D.C. area had to offer. It was a fantastic and rewarding experience. Since I had already lived in the area and was familiar with the surroundings, I jumped on the opportunity to be assigned to the Old Guard.

I arrived to the Old Guard in February of 2000 and was assigned to Bravo Company. The first few weeks were a whirlwind of meeting everyone and going through Regimental Orientation Program or ROP (pronounced like rope) training. I had to learn how to march the Old Guard way, carry my rifle the Old Guard way, and wear the uniform the Old Guard way. I even had to learn how to stand in a formation and at the position of attention the Old Guard way. Everything taught in basic training was thrown out the window. The Old Guard has its own standards, its own way of doing things—one of the many reasons this unit stands out from other Army units. I started out in Third Squad of Second Platoon, which was the company's casket platoon. We were the ones who folded the American flag during funerals for our nation's veterans at Arlington National Cemetery. First Platoon was the marching element and Third Platoon was the firing squad element for the 21-gun salute performed before Taps was played. Funeral detail rotated around Bravo, Charlie, and Delta companies of the Old Guard. There was Primary Week, Secondary Week and then a Training Week. The company responsible for Primary Week conducted all of the funerals for Arlington National Cemetery. Any funerals the Primary Company could not handle were sent to the company who was in their Secondary Week. There were typically one to four Full Honors funerals each day. Those funerals took the longest to perform because you loaded the casket on a horse-drawn caisson and marched alongside it to the soldier's final resting place. These funerals also had a marching element and band associated with them. Six-man funeral teams had more funerals to perform. Arlington National Cemetery had multiple funerals throughout the day from all branches of service.

I was initially assigned to a six-man casket detail. Six-man team funerals only had a firing squad and a bugle player for Taps, in addition to the casket team. I eventually made it to First Squad, which was the 8-man casket team reserved for Full Honors funerals. Full Honors funerals had a marching band, a separate marching element (1st Platoon, Bravo Company), a caisson element, the casket team, a firing squad, and of course a bugle player for Taps. Funerals were not the only role soldiers assigned to the Old Guard performed. I was fortunate enough to be a part of wreath laying ceremonies at the Tomb of the Unknown Soldier, parades for foreign dignitaries, cordons for the President of the United States, and several other special events.

Several special events stand out from all the others for me personally. I participated in the official opening ceremony of the Korean War Memorial, where I met President Bill Clinton. I personally escorted several Olympic athletes for the 2000 U.S. Olympic Committee dinner at Union Station. I was able to meet and talk with two women from the U.S Women's Soccer Team, a Gold medal gymnast, and a diver. All of them were gracious and honored that we were there and conversed with us about our unit and the military. True professionals. We ate dinner at Union Station and were able watch the entire event. After dinner, I took the U.S. Olympic Committee flyer left at each seating area on the tables and asked for several autographs from the Olympians. I still have this flyer in my cubicle at work. Somewhat faded now, but it seems like yesterday I was carrying on conversations with some of the more famous household names of Olympic athletes our nation has seen. Another event I was extremely fortunate to partake in was performing escort duties for former Medal of Honor recipients during the First Inaugural Address of President George W. Bush, in January 2001. The Medal of Honor recipients had special seating for the Inaugural Address just to the left of the podium in front of the U.S. Capitol.

The last event as an Old Guard soldier that stands out was the tradition of "Flags In," where we would place small American flags on every tombstone in Arlington National Cemetery. The tradition continues to this day. You loaded your ruck sack full of the small American flags, the same ones you would line your sidewalk or driveway with, and walk up and down the rows of the cemetery. One feels a tremendous amount of pride taking part in this tradition. Every Memorial Day weekend I come across news articles on social media detailing soldiers from the Old Guard taking part of this honored tradition. I never expected to be involved in so many of these special events. They were simply bonuses of being assigned to the Old Guard. Although these events were unique and extraordinary, none of them had such a life-changing significance as that of September 11, 2001.

The morning of Tuesday, September 11, 2001, was like most mornings at the Old Guard. We had our physical training formation, which coincided with Reveille, then of course physical fitness training. Following our workout, we ate breakfast at the chow hall then proceeded to prepare for squad/platoon meetings. We were in a training week during this time and not scheduled to perform any funerals in the cemetery. I remember hearing about the first plane hitting one of the World Trade Center towers while I was getting dressed on the third floor of the barracks. Without knowing any of the details, I assumed it was a small engine plane like a Cessna flying too low through clouds. I couldn't have been more wrong. A passenger airliner was unimaginable. I went on with my day preparing for the meetings not paying any further attention. A short time later, we heard another plane had hit the World Trade Center. Since we did not have a television on the third floor of the barracks, several of us rushed downstairs to the dayroom on the main floor of the barracks where we had a large projection-style television. Several others had already gathered in front of the television, which was tuned to one of the news channels. We hovered around murmuring to each other about what we were witnessing. I remember seeing fire and smoke from the towers billowing out. You know how events take place in the world and it seems surreal? That's the only way I can explain how I felt about what I was seeing. This was prior to the attack on the Pentagon. I felt so far removed from New York City. It didn't directly affect me. I didn't know anyone in New York, had never been there, and had no ties directly or indirectly to the city, the people, or even the professional sports teams. I was in disbelief that anything like this could have occurred, yet it still didn't affect me. I wonder today if this is what it was like for my grandfather and millions of other Americans who heard about the attack on Pearl Harbor or when Germany invaded Poland and continued their march throughout western Europe. I am not sure how long I watched the news and I can't even remember what news channel we were watching that morning. I do remember a platoon leader, who was so close to the big screen television pointing at the live newscast of the towers saying words to the effect of, "Everyone above this floor is dead." I was unsure about that. This was prior to both towers collapsing.

We were eventually told to head down to the conference room in the basement of the barracks for a meeting to discuss upcoming training events. I don't think we were in the meeting for more than five minutes before someone opened the conference room door and barged in, interrupting the meeting saying, "One-hundred percent accountability formation, right now! The Pentagon was just attacked!" It wasn't New York and it wasn't Pearl Harbor, this was across the street on Interstate 395. This was in my backyard! Now I really began to wonder what was going on. It scared me to think what was next...

Going back to my initial enlistment, I had only signed up for three years. Even though I had wanted to become an officer, by this time I began contemplating the idea of leaving the military and being done with my service in the summer of 2002. I was tossing around the idea of moving back to Texas and enrolling in the University of Texas in Arlington. I had an uncle who resided in Irving, Texas, and I thought about moving in with him. I had it all planned out in my head, but the events of 9/11 and the days following changed the course of my life and my military and professional career.

We rushed upstairs and assembled for accountability outside in the formation area in between Bravo and Delta Company. The two companies shared an "H" shaped building. I don't remember being told much other than First Platoon was ordered to go "full battle rattle," as they were being sent into Arlington National Cemetery near the boundary closest to the Pentagon to ensure no one was trying to hop the wall of Arlington and enter the cemetery. I don't recall everything that transpired that day, only a handful of events. I remember trying to call my Dad in New Mexico at one point to let him know I was all right. Later in the day, maybe early evening, I eventually was able to speak with my girlfriend. I told her I was all right and asked her to call my Dad and let him know I was fine. The phone lines and cellular networks were completely tied up and I was unable to place any calls. We eventually turned our attention back to the news and discovered at least one of the towers had collapsed. Later in the day, our squad leader had us conduct hip pocket training. Hip pocket training was really just random training on tactics or skills to reinforce training we had already received. I don't exactly remember what our hip pocket training was. I simply recall thinking we were just wasting time and that conducting the training was ridiculous. Three planes have hit buildings and landmarks in the U.S., and I wanted to keep watching the news to find out what was going on. At this point, I don't recall a fourth plane being involved in the day's events. I remember questioning my squad leader as to why we were doing hip pocket training. He told me we were going to conduct the training regardless. His tone and facial expressions were stern and non-negotiable, much like when I tell my children to do something and they rebel. Looking back now, I understand why we were conducting the training. We needed to be kept occupied and away from the television. We needed a reprieve from what was happening. As the day went on, I recall looking out the window from the third floor of our barracks and seeing two jet fighters, F-16s I believe, flying somewhat low around the city of Arlington. Low enough to tell they were fully armed and flying in a patrol-like manner. This image is still etched in my memory. I guess it was at this moment I realized things were different. Maybe the first time I thought that life would be forever changed.

We went on lock that day and spent the night in the barracks. It was unsettling to be placed on lockdown. There was so much uncertainty on the day's events and what the future would hold. We were not told how long lockdown would be. This only added to the uncertainty. You have to be flexible in the military. You have to learn to go with the flow and be able to adapt to the evolution of events. We used to say "Semper Gumbi," "Always Flexible!" It was our take on the U.S. Marine Corps saying of "Semper Fi," short for "Semper Fidelis," "Always Faithful!" The days and weeks ahead reinforced this statement. Dennis Brady and I were roommates at the time. We lived off-post in an apartment off Edsall Road in Alexandria. I think we used our Army issue sleeping mats and sleeping bags for when we conducted field training exercises. I think others shacked up with friends who lived in the barracks.

We were released the next morning to go home and rest and told to return later that afternoon. When we arrived back at the barracks in the late afternoon/early evening of September 12, we dressed in our Battle Dress Uniform (BDUs) and were transported by two-and-a-half ton ("deuce-and-a-half") Army trucks over to the Pentagon just outside of where Flight 77 had struck the west wing of the building. Many times, on our way to the Pentagon, motorists would honk their horns and wave at us as we rode down the highway. Multiple ambulances, police vehicles, and fire department trucks were all around that section of the Pentagon. The entire area was chaotic and a mess. Large floodlights illuminated the crash site. The strident voices of workers and machines were all around. It was overstimulating. I was seeing firsthand what had occurred and why we were put on lockdown. I saw a large section of the Pentagon missing. The famous images you can see now on the Internet with the roof collapsed, broken windows, and smoke billowing were right before my eyes. There were people everywhere working on rescue efforts.

Initially, we were split up into groups and went inside the Pentagon to assist with searching for survivors. We helped clear paths for other rescue workers and assisted with bringing out those who had been recovered. I don't recall exactly how many times I personally went inside the Pentagon or even how many days, but on several occasions, I entered to the left of the crash site. Our company had the night shift. Initially, we only wore our BDUs and Army-issued black leather gloves, along with a hardhat. We entered in and around the attack site wading through water and presumably jet fuel and other liquids. At times we were knee-deep in it while helping to clear out debris and searching. As I waded through the water and debris, I couldn't help but feel uncertain about my next step. We had to be cautious and take our time moving throughout the building. I personally never recovered one of the victims, but others with whom I served did. Debris was everywhere. Offices were in complete disarray. Sometimes fires broke out and we had to evacuate the Pentagon and wait for an all clear to reenter. There was a fear of walls and ceilings collapsing further. During one evening, a thunderstorm rolled through the area and we had to evacuate the staging area outside of where Flight 77 struck and enter the Pentagon to the right of the attack site to seek shelter from a suspected tornado, which did touch down in Maryland. I remember thinking, "What more could happen?" Here we were, frequently evacuating from inside the Pentagon because fires would break out or because there was a danger of the building further collapsing, and now we were seeking shelter inside the building from a tornado warning. We rotated in and out of the Pentagon often to give us much-needed breaks.

During one of my trips inside the Pentagon, I remember assisting with the removal of a section of landing gear from the airplane. During breaks, we stood watching everything that was going on. We simply waited for our next tasking. I don't think there was a soldier or a volunteer there who would have turned down any job asked of them. If they had told me to rappel down the roof and enter through a window, I would have done it without thinking twice. Sometimes we huddled together talking about what we experienced. Other times we told stories to simply pass the time during the early morning hours, the time of day during which our shifts ended.

We would then be transported back to Fort Myer, VA, to be released for the day and return late in the afternoon. We would hang up our BDUs and leave our combat boots out to dry out on the third floor of the barracks. This eventually produced a significantly foul stench in the room. After several repeated days of this, we started completely dressing in the full protection suits. The bleach-white body suits along with rubber gloves, boots, masks, and helmets. By now, decontamination areas had been established. When we were rotated out of the Pentagon, which happened quite often, we entered the decontamination area underneath a portable tent and proceeded to be washed and scrubbed down. As we exited the tent, we would remove our suits, scrub our rubber gloves and boots, and finally be done with the decontamination area. During one of these decontamination episodes, I recall seeing Secretary of Defense Donald Rumsfeld, along with members of his staff, walking around and surveying the progress of the recovery efforts. It was somewhat unexpected to see him there. I had only seen him hanging from an 8.5" × 11" frame on the wall with the rest of the Chain of Command photos.

Over the course of the next few days (or should I say nights?), we continued performing various jobs. Every night was filled with uncertainty. We all knew our jobs; however menial, were part of a much larger mission. I don't recall spending any abnormal length of time doing any one particular duty. Time really was not something I thought about. Maybe that is why only

Secretary of Defense Donald Rumsfeld (center) assesses the recovery effort while accompanied by Senators John Warner (right) and Carl Levin (left) (photograph by Helene C. Stikkel).

certain events and conversations stand out. The only monotonous time I had was guarding the hallways at night. You were removed from all the power generators, floodlights, and workers from the outside.

As the days continued, the response to the attacks grew. It seemed like every evening when we reached the Pentagon, there were more workers and volunteers. All the volunteers pulled together as one big family. Rescue efforts never stopped. Restaurants like Burger King, Outback Steakhouse, and several others began establishing mobile food stations to feed the responders. The Red Cross provided coffee and hot chocolate and friendly faces throughout the night. We had various duties throughout the next few weeks. We would be pulled from the recovery efforts and assigned to various other tasks. We guarded hallways inside the Pentagon to ensure no unauthorized personnel could access the offices located in the specific corridor. We assisted in collecting, packaging, and safeguarding classified information in an effort to clear areas that were no longer suitable to store such information, much less to even work in. We had to sign non-disclosure agreements, which are probably still binding to this day.

Eventually the American flag was draped over the side of the Pentagon for the entire world to see. Our flag was beautiful and there was tremendous pride in seeing our Stars and Stripes.

One of the final tasks I remember being assigned was patrolling the exterior perimeter of the Pentagon North Parking lot. This was the designated area for debris removal from the Pentagon to be unloaded and spread out in order for cadaver search dogs and personnel to sift through and potentially recover any human remains. German Shepherds and their handlers would meticulously search the debris for any signs of human remains. This was another one of those surreal moments that one can only experience and never truly describe to another. We patrolled and guarded the surrounding area several nights. Mainly, we were trying to prevent bystanders and vehicles from loitering around the area and taking photographs while the search for remains continued. It was during this task I recall speaking with a female Special Agent from the Federal Bureau of Investigation. She was from the FBI office in Minneapolis, if I'm not mistaken. I remember speaking with her about her background and about joining the FBI.

On October 6, 2001, one of the final tasks I performed with First Squad was conducting the Full Honors funeral service for the highest-ranking Army service member who died during the attack on the Pentagon. Our squad was tasked to perform the funeral for the three-star general and fold the American flag. The funeral was on a Saturday morning at Arlington National Cemetery, a rare event to be held on a Saturday. Television crews filmed the event, which was another rare aspect for a funeral. I knew it was special to be a part of that ceremony; however, given the circumstances at that time, it seems odd to say I was fortunate to have partaken in this funeral. The whole reason why we even performed this funeral to begin with was because of the terrorist attacks on our country.

Recall the girlfriend I had mentioned earlier? We had been dating for almost two months during this time. We officially met at a local Church of Christ congregation in Annandale, Virginia. She later told me that when 9/11 occurred, she knew she cared for me and hoped I was nowhere near the attacks given the proximity of my duty station. I eventually proposed and married her in 2002. Almost 17 years later, we still talk about how that Tuesday in September impacted our lives. After 9/11 and Operation Noble Eagle, I decided I was not ready to leave military service. I eventually reenlisted and became a Special Agent with the U.S. Army Criminal Investigation Division Command, commonly known as CID. CID is the Army's version of the FBI. I eventually left active duty service in 2008, serving just under 9 years. I crossed over from being an active duty CID agent and became a civilian CID agent, otherwise known by the federal employment series as an 1811. I continued working for the U.S. Army for a total of 19 years, active duty plus civil service. Since my first assignment in the military, I have lived in the D.C. area on one other occasion. As a civilian CID agent, I deployed three times, once to Iraq and twice to Afghanistan. During the tour in Iraq, I read *Decision*

Points by President Bush. Earlier, I referred to those surreal moments I experienced. This was again one of those moments. There I was serving as an E-4 Specialist assigned to one of the most prestigious units in the military folding our Nation's Flag for our fallen veterans. Then I'm standing in front of our nation's capital watching President Bush being sworn in. Honestly, I never should have been in the Old Guard. If Airborne School had been in my contract, or if I was allowed to be assigned to Fort Bragg, I would have said no to the Old Guard recruiter in Fort Benning, Georgia. Now here I was deployed to a country linked to 9/11 and reading the autobiography of the very same President whose first Inaugural Address I attended, reading about his account of the terrorist attacks that would see the Old Guard respond.

That fateful day in September altered the lives of so many and changed the direction of our nation. My story is not profound, heroic, or even extraordinary. Hopefully I've provided enough details (like a Bob Ross painting) for you to understand how unique the Old Guard was and is. How the events of a single day impacted my career, my life, and my family. It was an absolute honor to serve in this unit and for this nation. Our flag means so much to our great nation. I will not get political regarding our storied flag, especially with recent events. This is neither the time nor the place for that discussion. All I can tell you is on that day, and the days immediately following, our nation pulled together and our flags were everywhere. It seemed to be one of the most patriotic days in our country's history in the midst of tragedy.

The Impact of 9/11, Then and Now

WILLIAM ARTHUR ROUM

Life Before Joining the Military

My name is William A. Roum. On the surface, I was a normal kid who had a very similar story to a lot of small city or town men and women who turned 18 or just graduated from high school and joined the military. I was born in the small city of Dunkirk, New York, which is located on the shores of Lake Erie. This was also where the first shots of the War of 1812 occurred just off the beach. Dunkirk is roughly 20 miles from my reservation (the Cattaraugus Indian Reservation). My father was partially deaf and illiterate (because during that time in the educational system, children were just left behind) and worked in a radiator factory for most of his adult life. My mother was a seamstress who, after losing her job when her factory closed, began a journey to become a nurse while juggling the raising of four boys, attending school and working 20 miles away.

I was far from a model student and ended up being kicked out of high school shortly after my 18th birthday. I decided that instead of having the same life in the factory as everyone else's family, there had to be something better. My two eldest brothers joined the Marine Corps immediately after they graduated. But being me, I joined the Army on an Airborne Infantry contract.

I come from an extremely long lineage of warriors, I am a member of the Seneca Nation of Indians, which was a member of the Iroquois League/Confederacy. Our tribe has been fighting within North America long before it was given a name. We have fought proudly and sometimes hesitantly in every major conflict for the benefit of the U.S. Since the French and Indian War and the American Revolutionary War, my ancestors have been woven into the fabric of the United States through our military prowess, tactics (father of modern-day Guerrilla Warfare), and our diplomacy. Our Great Law of Peace was the foundation for the U.S. Constitution. I guess you can say I was made for the Infantry and bred for the military.

Arrival to the Old Guard

It was a snowy Thanksgiving eve in 2000 when I first arrived at Fort Myer, my first real duty station. The reason this day is so easy to recall for me is not that it was a snowy holiday, but for the fact that Fort Myer was a ghost town. Everyone was gone except for a few soldiers who had to be there for CQ (Charge of Quarters) and Staff Duty. My family had driven me through a snowstorm from my hometown of Dunkirk, New York, because I had decided to not utilize personal leave outside of Recruiter assistant duty (the Hometown Recruiting program).

Reporting for duty on a holiday was a nerve-racking experience for several reasons. Company assignments were based on numbers, not names. Upon my arrival, I literally did not have a company assignment. Much like a lottery system, it was all dependent upon which company CQ had open beds in their barracks and the order that each new soldier arrived.

These few days alone gave me an opportunity to reflect upon this new chapter in my life. So many questions were circling in my mind. Did I make the right career decision by turning down my contract to become a sky soldier with the 173rd Airborne unit in Vincenza, Italy? Was I meant to become a poster child for the U.S. Army? I made the decision against my initial intentions for the Military, I had met some great young men within my platoon during basic, and a small group of them decided to be recruited for assignment to "the Old Guard" (TOG). My Senior Drill Sergeant was a man whom I looked up to because he didn't entirely fill my ideal mold of what an Infantryman should look like, but still somehow proved worthy of my respect in every situation I saw him presented with.

I remember being instructed to grab my bags and follow the E-5 on duty to an older building that housed Bravo Company, whose layout was similar to what I can only think of as a college dorm. I was shown a room and told to get some rest but not to unpack because until the company returned from the holiday weekend and I was officially in-processed, I didn't have a home.

That same evening, Private Mongilutz showed up at some awful hour and turned on the lights in our temporary room. It was good to see a familiar face, just not at the time. I guess I had a funny way of showing my happiness during my youth. I remember linking up with another Private who was in our basic training unit and decided to go explore our new surroundings. But first we needed some new clothes before we hit the streets of Washington, D.C. This trip would lead to my first and only potentially harmful interaction with the Fort Myer Military Police.

On my maiden voyage through Rossyln, Georgetown, Pentagon City, and our national Capital, my fellow Warlords and I lost track of time and forgot that the back gate would close early because of the weekend gate hours in place. We must have walked 10–15 miles minimum that day. When we finally walked up the hill to Wright Gate, we were exhausted, and no one had enough money for a cab, let alone a cell phone. I don't recall who made the call, but one of us took charge and said, let's climb the wall. What we didn't take into account were the cameras pointed at that gate. Fewer than five minutes after clearing the walls, a couple of MPs pulled up with lights flashing. We were lucky that this was an older, more understanding MP, in that he was more focused on us not doing it again versus hauling us back to our company CQ desk. This would not have been a good foot to start on.

9/11 Attack and Time at the Pentagon

The morning of the 9/11 attacks started out like any typical day when Bravo Company was in the training portion of the regimental rotation. Third Platoon was waiting in the Quad for the day's training. If my memory serves me correctly, we were either donning riot gear or working on our ceremonial proficiencies. In any case, we were in the Quad waiting for senior leadership to join us. I am not sure of the correct order of the following events because that next month tends to be one long blur for me, but one of the Sergeants who was known for being a jokester yelled out from the dayroom that the World Trade Center just got bombed/attacked. Some of us dismissed this because we were already miserable from standing around waiting for training to begin. A few moments later, we heard an airliner fly really low overhead, low enough that we could hear the sounds from a jet pitching and rolling and slowing down. The reason this random occurrence sticks out is because planes didn't fly over Fort Myer. The predominant flight paths for the nearest airport, which is the Ronald Reagan Washington National Airport (DCA), is over the Potomac River. Some soldiers had initially thought this plane was going to crash into the *one* high-rise building on Fort Myer, which housed a good portion of the lower enlisted families.

Once leadership officially gave Bravo Company the word of what was actually occurring, we were given instructions to report back to our respective rooms to start grabbing our issued work gloves, Kevlar helmets, and some other items before standing by. This was one of the few times in my life in which time both stood still and flew by. We finally got the word to get into

A small piece of American Airlines 77 rests a short distance from the Pentagon (photograph by Journalist 1st Class Mark D. Faram, USN).

formation because our transportation was en route. We loaded the LMTVs and started making our way to the Pentagon where a lot of us were just trying to figure out what exactly to expect once we got onsite. We had run past the Pentagon for Physical Training (PT) or driven past it an infinite amount of times. Our barracks were only a few miles away. Upon our arrival, we witnessed a giant smoldering hole in the wall and tons of tents and agencies performing search-and-rescue. One of the first orders was to drop our gear in a Government tent adjacent to the crash (impact) site.

We were then divided by platoons and given different tasks ranging from providing security in various parts of the interior to helping out with various tasks in other areas. I recall the severe lack of protective equipment we were given to wear in the first few days. We were given construction masks and goggles along with our Kevlar (helmets) and work gloves (standard issue leather). The primary mission during the beginning was the retrieval of remains and putting large plane parts in a couple of piles. A few days into this mission, we were made to wear full Tyvek suits, rubber boots, duct tape around the wrists and ankles, and a full mask. When we exited out of the wreckage to eat, rest, or change shifts, we would have to go through decontamination tents. We could rest and sleep and eat in the tent adjacent to the crash site. It was just as confusing then as it is now as to why it was okay to sleep in a tent which was only a hundred or so feet away from the site with no protective gear, while we had to be in full Tyvek suits when at the crash site. I never found out what we were breathing in.

Working within the crash site was brutal in so many ways. Physically, we were constantly rotating between rest, eating, and helping retrieve remains and plane parts as well as helping to clear debris. Mentally and emotionally, things are still rough to look back on. A soldier really didn't have time to fully contemplate what they were actually doing. Sifting through the wreckage and coming across a burnt family photo, a wallet, a small piece of a child's toy, or even body parts. One moment that has left mental scarring and a lasting impact on my life occurred one night shortly after the attacks when a body was found under some debris. We attempted to remove the body and place it in a bag for removal from the site, but when trying to lift the body by the legs and arms, the flesh and muscles started peeling back from the bone. To this day I won't eat anything with a bone on it, and I won't eat things like steak. Mentally I can't, I try to even avoid watching others eat and remove a large bone. I think that being in the Old Guard and doing countless funerals helped numb my emotions during that time of my life. I believe that numbness really helped back then.

It was pretty easy for someone to lose track of time back then, more so now, while looking back. I don't remember how many days we were at the Pentagon, I feel as if it were somewhere around a month. When we weren't at the Pentagon, we were augmenting the Military Police (MPs) by helping inspect vehicles entering Fort Myer. That time in my life really was just one giant blur.

Post–9/11 Attack

Once the pace of things slowed down, Bravo Company fell back into the standard three-week rotation of Primary, Back-up, and Detail. When we were on detail week, we would still help inspect vehicles entering Fort Myer. Just over a year later, the National Capital Region (NCR) would be under attack again. This time it was initially thought to be random attacks, but quickly turned into something far worse. This series of shootings, carried out by two males (41-year-old John Allen Muhammad and 17-year-old Lee Boyd Malvo) did all but stop operations around D.C. I recall being told on certain days to keep the curtains closed, and some who lived off-post were encouraged to stay at the barracks. There was so much misinformation being put out to the public at this time. During all the shootings, people all reported seeing a white work van. The problem with this is there must be thousands and thousands of white work vans in the Metro Area. I bet almost 90 percent of local contractors had white vans. After the D.C. Snipers were caught, the remainder of my time in the Old Guard was very smooth. I was assigned to Special Details during the rest of my contract. By default, I ended up being in charge of performing off-post funerals within a two-hour radius and was then assigned to escort the Arlington Ladies to funerals they attended in Arlington National Cemetery (ANC).

After my ETS in June of 2003, I began working as a pharmacy technician and joined the U.S. Army Reserve as a Counterintelligence Agent. I decided that this position was not for me and ended up transferring to an Infantry unit. I joined the Virginia Army National Guard in December of 2003. I went to my first drill in Manassas along with a fellow Old Guard member (Fiske). We had no real expectations when we drove there. We were initially assigned to a platoon which was waiting for their new Drill location to be finished (we were referred to as NOVA platoon). We sat around most of Friday and Saturday, not accomplishing much. Was this what the National Guard was like? Why weren't we doing P.T., why weren't we training, why were we just sitting here? On Sunday, we finally got to meet with the Company First Sergeant. He asked us, "How was Active Duty?" and "Did you like it?" We both agreed it was pretty good to us. He then said, "I am glad you liked it, because you boys are going right back on Active." We had just found out that our new unit A Co. 3/116th had just received orders to deploy to Afghanistan. Our Deployment consisted of pre-mobilization at Ft. Bragg, N.C., home of the 82nd Airborne Division and the Green Berets. To better prepare for our Deployment, we did numerous road marches, P.T. tests, live-fire drills; this is where I had a Machine Gun Optics explode in my right eye, which I thought would cost me some of my eyesight.

Finally, we started prepping for actual Deployment, I remember having to stand in formation on a giant weight machine so we could get flight assignments. We had one final weekend with our respective families, then boarded the plane. I was so pumped to finally be on a plane heading overseas. I had been waiting for the opportunity to deploy to Afghanistan for three years, I had witnessed firsthand the carnage and damage done on 9/11. This was my chance for a "payback." Not to go too far down this road, but I served alongside of a lot of great men during this 18-month Deployment. I keep in touch with a few via texts and social media. Occasionally we share the humorous stories of dumb things we did or pranks we pulled on each other during downtime. Every now and then, we share some horrific tales as well as a way of coping or allowing a battle buddy to vent if they need help dealing.

Sometime after our return, we went back to our respective drill halls, and life went on.

I was later MEB boarded out.

During the first month back stateside, I started a career as a Government Security Contractor and continued that career for the next 13 years. I have recently rediscovered my want to work within the healthcare industry and plan on getting back into school and working toward a PharmD degree.

How 9/11 Changed My Views

Throughout the years, my feelings and opinions of the world have changed multiple times on several topics, ranging from religion to patriotism. Immediately following the attacks, I really didn't know how else to explain my thoughts besides through sheer anger. I didn't really know or understand my emotions at the time, and I really did not question them. I used to be a man who let his emotions guide him.

Approximately three years after my returning from overseas, I moved away from D.C., away from the memories, away from having to drive past the Pentagon on an almost daily basis. I ended up moving to Colorado in the summer of 2008. I think that having the feeling of being a world away was therapeutic for my soul to some extent. All my anger began to be suppressed the more time I spent in nature. My anger slowly changed to regret. I regretted not doing more to help while I was in Afghanistan. Was my time there spent to the benefit of that country? I mean, we accomplished all the missions handed down, to include aiding and securing that country's historic first democratic election. But could we have done more? Were more teachers shot or killed because they were attempting to teach little schoolgirls? Were any more women and children killed because they wanted to learn? All these things randomly cross my mind from time to time. This usually occurs when news about Afghanistan pops up in the media. I wonder what happened to Ghazni and the surrounding villages. I know that in the last few years, the Taliban overran our old Forward Operating Base (FOB Ghazni).

After moving around the country for almost 12 years, I have finally settled down in Castle Rock, Colorado, with my family. I have learned to accept things that have happened to me as a result of being a first responder. It is my burden alone to carry. I continually strive to suppress these things so I can an attempt to have a sense of normalcy and lead a decent life. But sometimes the thoughts creep back in, the nightmares come back, and you just have to wait for the storm to pass.

I strive to live by the words of Charles Swindell, who said, "We cannot change the inevitable. The only thing we can do is play on the one string we have, and that is our attitude…. I am convinced that life is 10% what happens to me and 90% how I react to it. And so it is with you… we are in charge of our attitudes." All in all, I am proud of everything I have done or been a part of as it relates to my time in the military. I am honored that I was recruited into the Old Guard, I am continuously humbled by my duties. Although some things have left me with unwanted mental scars, I would never change one minute from my service alongside my battle buddies.

We Laughed

Brett (Thurman) SanPietro

Third platoon was outside in the quad, practicing civil disturbance ops (riot control). It was routine and lighthearted. The closest we ever got to having actual riot control duty in D.C. was when, from our perspective, a bunch of tree-hugging, long-haired hipsters decided they wanted to protest a World Bank meeting. That's how we saw the world, anyway, collectively with the average age and world experience of a 20-year-old with maybe a few college courses and little or no time spent outside the United States. But hey, we were infantry. We volunteered, we did the hard jobs no one else could handle. So, of course, we felt justified in looking down on protestors, despite knowing nothing about them or for, that matter, much about the World Bank either.

But I digress...

So, everyone is getting fitted into their gear. The typical locker room-style talk and pranking you would expect. One guy whacks another in his armored chest with a riot baton, another smacking his buddy on the helmet with his body shield. It was a beautiful morning—I recall that with absolute certainty. Then, as we're getting formed up, the Charge of Quarters Sergeant (the guy whose job it is to basically sit at the front desk, greet visitors, and watch CNN all day—bored out of his mind) walks by, "Hey, guys, someone flew a plane into the World Trade Center."

"Shit, what an idiot asshole move," I recall thinking. I mean, that's where many of our minds immediately went. Probably one of those rich idiots who thought it would be a good idea to get their adrenaline rush with a private pilot's license. Screwed up in some major way. We all laughed about how big of a fuck up you had to be to miss something the size of a skyscraper. We didn't really have any details, so we jumped to what our minds most wanted to envision—someone better off than us screwing up royally. What an ass he must have been. What a bunch of asses *we* were.

We laughed. Damn, that's rough to think about now.

I want to take a beat here and provide some context. Talk about my fellow soldiers and give you some insight. You all know what comes next in the story, anyhow; I assume you'll suffer me a brief segue.

You probably already have some concept of what it is to be an Army Infantryman. Running, jumping, guns, and mud … that sort of thing. That's fine. Thanks to more recent written and film endeavors, some of you also have probably glimpsed more of the truth: it's 95 percent sitting around being bored, getting yelled at, and playing Xbox (our generation's iteration on a deck of cards). It's also 5 percent being scared shitless, doing things you might later get a medal for, but you can't honestly recall why you did it or what you were thinking in the moment, and ultimately just existing in a state of pure adrenaline rush that has got to be on par with being high in some way (though I honestly lack the life experience with other drugs to validate that comparison).

The Old Guard was different. Unique, even. Sure, we were infantry soldiers. And we trained to standard and I would later learn after seeing more of the Army, often well above the standard. But our primary mission was funerals. We put people in the ground. *Our* people.

We provided the marching escort, the firing party (21-gun salute), and the casket bearers ("Ma'am, on behalf of a grateful nation … here's your flag") for the funerals in Arlington National Cemetery (ANC). This meant that, technically, we didn't deploy (more on that later). Our place was in Arlington, and our job was death. Fitting, I suppose—in infantry training the drill sergeants always yell at you, all these mottos and maxims about death … platoons nicknaming themselves "Death Dealers." We just *dealt* with it on the back end. Most days, about three or four times a day, we laid a fellow soldier to rest.

Most of the time, it was an old retired veteran. Not at all like us. He was old; we'd never grow old. This guy did his tour in Vietnam or Korea, maybe a peacetime soldier, started collecting his pension and then eventually something else got him. Old age, diabetes, heart condition … all stuff we felt immune to. But other times … sometimes there were training accidents. A special operations mission gone wrong. We would put other 20-year-olds in the ground. And on the surface, it didn't affect us at all. On the surface, we were joking. Helicopter crash and they didn't recover any completely recognizable bodies? That was simply a "fingers and toes" mission. It wasn't meant in disrespect. Shit, we didn't even laugh most times. It just was what it was. It's how we dealt. And whenever we did bother to be a little introspective about it, we were all confident that our infantry brothers, the very ones we were laying to rest, would probably use the same slang and tell the same jokes over our bodies if the tables were turned. It's just how we were. It's how we were trained to be. Whistling through the graveyard. Sometimes literally.

So anyway, yeah, the morning of September 11, we laughed. In the moment it was because we lacked context, context that would come crashing down on us literally in minutes. But it's important that I share; it's who we were. We laughed at death, our own and also, sadly, others. Not out of bravado. Perhaps, ultimately, out of necessity. It's who we were. In some ways, I often reflect with some sadness, it's who I still am. But that can wait.

Fewer than 20 minutes later, the second plane hit. We were done with riot control practice at that point. We were done with whatever we thought the day would hold. Let's be honest, we were done living in the world we thought we knew.

A lot happened in the course of the next few hours; I'm sure my recollections are now biased and clouded by attempted reconstructions and chats with friends. They locked down the base. We drew our weapons from the arms room. They were talking about defending the base. Literally, physically, defending a U.S. base on U.S. soil. How surreal is that? There was some confusion. An entire base of military minds, trained to take initiative, apostles of the oft misquoted "In the absence of further orders…. Attack!" mindset, all trying to figure out what to do next. No one knew what exactly was happening and, perhaps worse, no one knew how we could help.

Everything cleared up about 30 minutes later.

American Airlines Flight 77 hit the Pentagon at 9:37 a.m. For me and those around me, it was something like a thud. Funny, any one of us could hear a loud or sharp bang and identify for you whether it was from a firecracker, a rifle, a pistol, or some type of artillery. Some of our guys could even tell you what type or size of artillery. We had just never before heard the sound of a few terrorists successfully attacking the physical embodiment of the U.S. military and forever changing the course of history.

The impact point on the Pentagon was about 1.5 miles from our Bravo Company barracks, as the crow flies. That hypothetical crow would fly directly over ANC, "the Garden," as we called it. We would later hear from some of our brothers in Delta Company, who had responsibility for funerals that morning, pieces of debris literally landed near them in the Garden. I can't tell you whether it's true, though I've got no reason to doubt them. Much of life as a low-ranking infantryman is what you hear from the guys on your left and right.

So now it was clear, right? We knew what we had to do. Terrorist attacks on a civilian target in New York, that requires thinking and logistics and talk about how to get units there and what units are best prepared to respond. But someone flies a plane into the Pentagon, that's a pretty clear-cut scenario. Or so it seemed to a bunch of 20-year-old infantrymen.

It wasn't until later in the day that we loaded up on the trucks. My brothers recall better than I do what happened up to this point. I'll leave that telling to them. I know at some point I got to my phone in my barracks room and changed my outgoing voicemail message to something along the lines of "… I'm ok, we're all ok, I probably won't be able to return your call for a while or a few days but I'll call when I can." I know this because hearing that message is what my dad still recalls to this day. It surely wasn't my idea. Our leadership wasn't stupid, they knew the calls would be pouring in and we didn't have time to deal with the outside world right now.

The next thing I remember is being on the back of an open-top two-and-a-half-ton truck with about 30 of my brothers and I crawling through traffic on Richmond Highway. Crawling along the shoulder, even with a police escort (Were they escorting us, or just already there?). Anyone who tells you the 9/11 attacks were staged doesn't have a clue what 9 a.m. traffic is like on the interstate and two highways wrapped around the Pentagon. It took us at least 30 minutes before we got to the crash site.

I remember this clearly because we were all singing "Build Me Up Buttercup."

We had a guy in our company, kind of the resident jokester. Always in trouble. The kind of guy I always thought I would be like, based on my high school experience, but then of course the Army changed me. But this guy, the Army didn't change him the way it did me. Whenever we were at our lowest, he'd sing. On our way out to do a patrol, in the rain, 35 degrees and dark, he'd just belt out at the top of his lungs "WHY DO YOU BUILD ME UP?" and we'd all call back the response. So, of course, on our way to the Pentagon, hours after terrorists attacked our nation, killed thousands of civilians, and ensured we would likely never know true peace again in our lives, we sang. We had gone from whistling through our graveyard, to literally singing as we drove past it.

I apologize. I haven't really taken the time to introduce myself. I suppose that's the least I could do before I ask you to come with me further. Honestly, I know my own story pretty well and perhaps I should share that with you before I ask your patience in dealing with the holes in my memory regarding the rest of my time at the Pentagon. It's funny what we choose to remember and what seems foreign, even when our trusted friends who were there with us at the time, recall it for us. So, allow me to digress again and perhaps build your assurance that I seek only to share the story as truly as I can recall.

I didn't join until I was 19. I graduated high school with something short of a 3.0, blessed by supportive parents and a parochial school education but held back by a general unwillingness to put in hard work on anything I didn't find interesting. One of those kids who would usually get straight As, but then in some subjects get the dreaded "Does not apply himself" note sent home. By the time I hit senior year, I was already mentally checked out, had a well-paying job, and figured I would work for a year or two until I could pay to go to college for acting. Yeah, I was the drama geek in high school. Didn't really find much else interesting.

After a year of making more money than a 19-year-old should and spending most of it, I took a look around and knew I needed a drastic change. I grew up in the Detroit area and it wasn't uncommon in my peer group for friends to go to community college, vocational schools, or perhaps work and go to college part-time on the way to completing a degree in six or seven years. In the words of that magic 8-ball, my outcome did "not look good." My friend and I were working on my car and went to the store for some parts. There just happened to be a recruiting station next door.

I signed up on an Airborne Ranger contract. I'd go to Fort Benning, attend 14 weeks of basic and infantry training, three weeks of Airborne School, and then go to a Ranger Regiment where I would inevitably lead a very difficult life until I was sent to Ranger School to earn my tab after 61 days of hell. As a 102-pound scrawny white kid from Detroit who didn't even play sports in high school, that sounded like a drastic enough change for me.

Friends were supportive but worried. No one else in my family or friend group had much experience with the military. Google was just starting to gain prevalence and one friend looked up the requirements for Ranger School and simply asked "Are you sure you can do this?" Mom was supportive but quiet. Dad, once he did his research, wasn't at all pleased. At one point offering to empty out his meager 401k in an attempt to match "whatever they offered" me. To their credit, since then they've all been there for me to this day, family and friends. They've been the memory in the back of my head when I've been freezing outside at night or scared for my life in some way. And, to leap ahead, they were there for me when I came home. They never judged me, even when they couldn't understand me. They welcomed me home, they held me, they even loved me when I completely failed to understand them and their world. I couldn't have asked for better.

Let's skip ahead. The Old Guard, the Army unit responsible for funerals in Arlington National Cemetery, the official escort to the President of the United States, is an infantry unit first and foremost. You don't get randomly assigned like most units. Mid and senior level leaders, officer and enlisted, all must apply. Junior soldiers, new recruits, are handpicked. Selected, based on a few quantifiable criteria (test results and height and weight measurements, mostly) plus the purely subjective opinion of a single Old Guard Sergeant, assigned to sit at Fort Benning and literally look at all the new infantry recruits coming in. As it happens, the Sergeant with this duty when I came through Fort Benning had a bias toward selecting kids with high test scores who had volunteered for the hardest possible gig (Airborne Ranger) and looked like they had absolutely no business being there (102 pounds and scrawny).

"Hey, Private, you're not going to Ranger Battalion anymore. You're going to the Old Guard. You know what the Old Guard is? Here, go over to the payphone and call your mom and tell her you're going to a non-deployable unit. You'll make her day."

You don't really get much say. Sure, it's a volunteer unit, but find me one fresh-off-the-bus Army enlistee willing to tell a Sergeant, who walks around Fort Benning like no one can tell him what to do, "No." So, I reported to Fort Myer in Arlington in February of 2000.

I made friends. I got stronger (it was a low bar to start from). I was actually starting to do pretty well for myself and was even working toward a shot at being selected to go to Ranger School (you can still go from units other than a Ranger Battalion, slots are just harder to come by). Two of the friends I made that year would stand up at my wedding 18 years later. Another three would attend and reminisce about old times after not talking for over a decade. If you don't have a friend who you can go without speaking to for ten years but can then call up and ask for a place to crash and to borrow a couple hundred dollars, I feel for you. Or maybe my norm just isn't the societal norm. Some of us went through hell together, or even hells, sometimes just in our own minds. Why did we go so long without talking? Maybe we were busy, maybe we're lousy friends by other standards, or maybe we just couldn't stand being reminded of who we were and what we did. But we're getting better, and we'll always be there for each other.

Ok, so where were we before I again went off track? In the truck, right? Belting out the repetitive chorus (never a verse) of "Build Me Up Buttercup." Well, we eventually got to the Pentagon. And here's where I stray from facts I would swear to, to memories as I recall them.

The plane struck the west side of the Pentagon. A lot has already been written about some of the fortunate coincidences (recent constructions, minimal staff presence) that contributed to keeping the casualty count low. Here's what I recall.

I could see their offices. Literally. The plane tore a massive gash in the side of the building. Charred concrete, some parts of the building still on fire, and offices you could look into like a cutaway drawing in a student's textbook. I could see someone's desk, their coat stand with a coat and hat still hanging on it. But no chair. The chair had been on the other side of the room. The side that was no longer there. The coat didn't have a scratch or burn mark on it. The room's occupant ... well, there was no way of knowing for sure.

There was also the helipad. You see, there was a helicopter landing pad on this side of the building and, as it was explained to us, the plane struck the ground right near the pad before then plowing forward into the Pentagon. "How about that, the pilot sucked at both landings" immediately came out the mouth of one of our guys. We all chuckled a bit. No one flat-out laughed. Never mind the actual intent, never mind the deaths or the still-burning building and what we would soon be facing inside. We still had our jokes. So inappropriate. So necessary.

This next part I'm sure didn't play out exactly how I recall, but I do think I've pieced it together from other facts I heard that day. Again, our life was defined by what we heard. From up top, for sure, but mostly from what we heard from the guy to our left and right.

We were told we were part of the rescue effort. Most people had been evacuated, but we still didn't know for sure. Something about parts of the building are still on fire, so engineers can't go in. But the structure might be unsound, so firefighters can only go so far. We were told there might still be people in there. You might not know this about the military: we're pretty big on accountability. You always know exactly how many people you have, at all times. We didn't have a good count. Or so we were told.

I remember reading about the dogs used for recovery efforts in New York. Rescue personnel would from time to time have to pretend to be an unconscious person, so the dog would experience a successful recovery and not get depressed at all the unsuccessful attempts, "recovering" only dead.

There are two for sure, never fail ways to get an infantryman to do something: (1) tell him it's too hard or dangerous for others to do, (2) tell him someone's been left behind. We're not alone in this, most of our military brothers and sisters (a subtle head-nod to my Marine colleagues here) will respond the same way. Given those two prompts, you could ask anything of us. These are the things we were told and the things we told each other and ourselves. I'm sure we didn't have the whole truth. But really, we didn't need it. A soldier seldom does. We had a mission; that was enough.

We went into the Pentagon wearing our Kevlar helmets, leather gloves, and Battle Dress Uniform (BDUs)—the green and black camouflage of the period. After a day or two, we got rebreather masks with filters, like painters wear. A couple days later, full Tyvek suits and yellow boots we would seal to each other with duct tape. The Old Guard (as I understand it) maintains to this day that we had full protective equipment prior to first entering the Pentagon. This simply isn't true. I can't attest to the actual timeline; I just know that we went in there without any extraordinary gear at all those first few days. I highlight this not to score political points but rather to remind you. Picture it: a fractured Pentagon, rubble, all sorts of waste, and a lack of assurance regarding structural stability. And batches of young men, 20-year-olds, walking straight inside without any hesitation. Just because it was the thing to do. The thing that had to be done.

The rescue effort (if this label ever applied to us) quickly gave way to a recovery effort. It lasted weeks. Our leadership would at times give us common sense guidance, which, in our sleep-deprived stupor, seemed a brilliant revelation. "Hey, guys, I know you only have six hours before you need to be back here but take a shower in the barracks before you get home. You don't ... don't take this shit home with you."

Once, upon exiting the Pentagon, we struck up a conversation with one of the technicians at the decontamination tent. It was his job to hose us down before we discarded our Tyvek suits and went back to our tent to catch a nap after a few hours of slogging around in the wreckage. "Hey, man, what exactly is it that you're spraying off of us here?" "Oh, all sorts of stuff, really. Definitely jet fuel, probably asbestos, a fair amount of human waste and remains..." Someone made a joke. I don't recall it exactly but, of course it happened. What else do you do in this situation other than laugh about it?

Let me take a beat to pause and focus on something a bit more uplifting. In the days immediately following the attack, the ground surrounding the Pentagon transitioned into something akin to a painfully somber and sleep-deprived county fair. Sure, we had fire and EMS and police and military personnel there. But we also had a Burger King trailer. Starbucks showed up with a table and volunteers at first, later, a full mobile coffee shop. There was a tent where you could get a 15-minute massage, provided (I assumed) by local community volunteers. That's just the part I remember, and I'm not a good source. I was either sleeping or waist deep in jet fuel and wreckage most of the time. But it was all there, free for all of us, as a community. Not everyone could put on a uniform and walk into the Pentagon but, dammit, whoever that kid was who put my Whopper together and handed it to me at 3 a.m., in the 30-minute window I had between decontamination and passing out for a few hours... that kid was my hero. Kid, shit, he was probably older than I was, now that I think of it.

There was press, as well. They kept a respectful distance and they certainly weren't my problem. Still, they wanted to talk to soldiers. Get their soundbites, hear from the "first responders" in person. So, every now and then the commander would send two or three of us up with the public affairs officer to the area where the press were permitted to gather. One woman was speaking with me, holding a microphone, and in the course of her questions asked how much longer we would be working here. I told her we'd be here until we were done... and she kind of choked up and said something about how touching that was. I didn't understand it at the time. She was looking for, she wanted, a timeline. When would this all end and be behind us? I couldn't see the bigger picture she was talking about; I was just talking about the mission. Ask any soldier when they're going home, odds are they'll tell you "when the mission is done." It's amazing how patriotic and self-sacrificing we can be when we don't actually know there's another option.

I think that's just about all I have to say about the days immediately following the attack. I apologize if it's not as full of a picture as you were looking for. Those are just the parts I care to remember and can truthfully share. Yes, it was horrible. We found people, parts of people, and sometimes the worst was when we found only the evidence that people had been ... the random teddy bear or just a single shoe. Shit ... that teddy bear.

Anyway, it'd be disingenuous if I focused on those parts of this experience. They aren't the ones that stick in my head. I remember the guys next to me. I remember sleep-deprived drives back to the house just to shower and crash for three hours in a bed and not on the floor. I remember our community coming together. And, if we're honest, I remember laughing. That pained, forced laughter that had no place in that sad and terrible world, other than to be our sole salvation.

I'm older now, as, of course, we all are. And probably I'm a bit wiser, too. The Old Guard did actually deploy not long after the attacks, in 2003. After which I followed through on my initial goal and got out of active service and went to college. September 11 always followed close behind me, even if I wasn't consciously aware of it. It would come up in conversation sometimes as an aside but then dominate the rest of the discussion. Some teacher or fellow student would talk about where they were. It means something a little different for all of us and I came to understand that. For my part, there are only a handful of people in this world I can speak with who understand what it meant for me. We're there for each other, whenever necessary.

I've had some more personal experiences with death since those days. A couple of friends. A few grandparents. Sooner or later it will be my own parents. And I feel sorely lacking in the moment. It's hard for me to share the emotion, the anguish, or surprise, or loss. I understand it, but ... it's just death. It seems so ... common, I suppose. It's something I'm working on. Painfully ironic, that someone would work on feeling more emotionally wracked over something. No one tries harder to be heartbroken when their partner breaks it off with them....

I've maintained some level of service ever since. First with the National Guard, then as a diplomat with the State Department, and now with the Navy Reserves. It turns out, it can be hard to get much meaning out of life when you don't have a mission. I used to think adrenaline was the only drug the Army got you hooked on. Now I think that was just the gateway.

When I think back on that day, as I get older, I am most fixed on the reality that we haven't known a day of true peace since. Closing in on 20 years now. I don't have anything much more profound than that to share. I just think it's worth remembering and talking about. How long are we going to live like this, in a constant state of smoldering war that slowly burns at the edges of a life we once knew?

America on Fire: A Grunt's Perspective

ROBERT EARL WILLIAMS

My Origins as an Oxygen Thief

My name is Robert Earl Williams, and I am a grateful veteran of the United States Army, the finest military machine the world has ever known. Most folks call me Bob, but for a treasured and meaningful time in my life, the people closest to me called me "Squirrel." To reveal the origin of that nickname would be incongruous with the good nature of most self-respecting citizens. Suffice to say, the moniker was associated with my enthusiastic fondness for the fairer sex.

Back to the subject at hand, shall we? Inspired by my West Point–grad dad, I almost always envisioned myself serving our country. I had dreamed of triumphantly mirroring his accomplishments, pinning on lieutenant's bars while wearing cadet gray with the Hudson River in the background and the flag flying in the breeze overhead.

That wasn't in the cards, I'm afraid.

Born in 1976 in Scottsdale, Arizona (a most comfortable place to grow up, to be sure), I was child number four of five, with parents who divorced much earlier than any boy would like. Although my childhood wasn't exactly idyllic, I can't complain about the overall experience. My former West Pointer, Air Force captain dad transitioned to executive with a prominent tech company in New Zealand, where I spent much of my teen years, plotting the next phase in life.

West Point was soon out of the question. As a result of life overseas, I lacked participation in the requisite stateside admission events. More importantly, I have to concede that my academic achievements were too pedestrian for such an elite academy.

Plan B found me enrolling at Arizona State University, joining the four-year ROTC program so as to achieve the same result and pin on those "butter bars," just in a less acclaimed institution. A *lot* less acclaimed.

Look, there are worse places to spend a college career than Tempe, Arizona. ASU boasted a wide array of recreational distractions, to put it mildly. I spent about a year-and-a-half in ROTC but found myself derailed by a foe that bested many a man and Sun Devil before me: alcohol. Booze, attractive women and the bright lights of the nation's Number One Party School derailed the mission I had planned well over a decade earlier. Withdrawing from ROTC, I decided to pursue a business career in the private sector; if I couldn't be disciplined and heroic, I might as well be rich. So, I rallied, and graduated with a Bachelor's in Business Management in only three years, all while working full-time, learning the craft—and craftiness—of sales. Determined to set the world on fire with a deftness of skill and drive that would rival the fictitious Gordon Gekko, I would find riches and success in the corporate world or die trying!

The outpouring of money and a meteoric rise to the exclusive mahogany and leather offices of the corporate penthouse were a wee bit harder to achieve than I had anticipated. However, after a hardscrabble, post-collegiate year of skipping breakfast and scarfing Top Ramen in a barren apartment, I did carve out a respectable role in the business world. I became an Account Executive at a technology firm, hawking computer hardware to emerging companies in the newly birthed E-commerce economy. I was good at it, and there was a discernible path to success ahead. Bob Williams climbed a slow-but-steady, achievable Corporate American ladder. So maybe I wouldn't get rich, but I would be comfortable if I continued my plodding gait.

A funny thing happened then. In November of 1999, I found myself staring at my computer monitor after having hung up the phone with a client and caught a glimpse on the newfound internet of American soldiers in Kosovo and the Baltic Regions, "keeping the peace." I instantly recalled my eight-year-old self being discovered in my father's closet, his cadet gray uniform drooped over my little shoulders, blaring John Phillips Sousa on a record player and brimming with patriotism and love of country. A powerful question struck me hard as lightning: "Is this as meaningful as your existence will ever get?"

I contemplated a life of simply pursuing success in business and considered whether that would be fulfilling enough for me to be at peace when I close my eyes for the final time. The answer was a resounding no. Those same apple pie, Fourth of July flyovers at baseball games feelings relit a fire inside of me that had been there all along, but just barely flickering like a pilot light. It was time to fulfill my destiny and join the military. Only now I wouldn't have the privilege of pinning on officer rank. That ship had sailed with only me to blame. However, I could still make a meaningful difference and fulfill the mandate of my own conscience. America was the greatest nation in the history of the world, and I would do my part to serve Her.

Branch of service wasn't much of a deliberation. The Marines love to brag that they are the best, but their 14 weeks of basic training are identical to the time spent by an infantry soldier in the Army. Oh, and if you want to get a rise out of a Marine ask him or her where they go for paratrooper training. (Spoiler! The answer is the U.S. Army Post at Fort Benning.) Don't forget to throw in the fact that the Army has made more amphibious landings than the Marines, and you have a recipe for an explosive but amusing reaction. They also wear odd, crown-like covers (hats), and sandwich the word "sir" at the beginning and ending of every sentence, even to non-officers. Very polite! They do have great commercials though, slaying dragons and whatnot. I tease in good fun, but in reality, the Marines are a fine institution. They just weren't for me.

The Air Force is uniquely an officer's service branch. Nearly every other branch sends enlisted men into the fray, but not the Air Force. The officers there do the fighting as pilots. The Navy has a combination of officer/enlisted warriors, but 95 percent of the people the Air Force sends into harm's way wear brass. Unfortunately, a commission at that point in my life was not an option. Respectable as it is, I didn't fancy a life of maintaining aircraft equipment or waving orange batons on a tarmac. The Air Force was out.

And remember, my father went to West Point. After watching ONE Army-Navy football game with him as a kid, I swiftly determined the Navy could NEVER be an option. Not if I wanted to have peaceful holiday dinners. Need I say more?

The United States Army was inevitable. The remaining question was what job would I select? Which Military Occupational Specialty (MOS) would I find myself serving in? I was off to my local recruiting station.

After completing the Armed Services Vocational Aptitude Battery (ASVAB), my recruiter suggested air traffic controller, translator and a couple other positions, all requiring six-year commitments. I balked. What if I had erred in my judgment to join and six years turned out to be an interminable sentence? And in truth, I arrogantly fancied myself the next Audie Murphy or Sergeant York. I inquired as to whether or not I could enlist in the Infantry for only a minimal three-year commitment. The recruiter had the paperwork out before I even finished my sentence.

On February 23, 2000, I took the oath of enlistment at the Phoenix Military Entrance Processing Station. My sister delivered me to said location, and my last sense of civilian life was her yelling, "Keep a stiff upper lip, Bobby!" as an elevator door closed in my face.

"Basic" Deficiencies

Basic training was very much the way it is depicted in the movies. Drill sergeants scream at you to the point of hoarseness. They make you feel worthless only to build you back up again. You rarely get meaningful sleep, hunger is perpetual, and you second guess your decision to join 90 percent of every day. My experience was very similar to the stereotype with one notable exception—the lack of heavy weapons training, essential for every infantryman.

When you place 44 young men in a barracks the size of a horse corral and keep them there for 14 weeks, even the sternest of immune systems has trouble keeping pace. Thus Bob "Squirrel" Williams, America's next super soldier, became deathly ill mid-cycle and was hospitalized for an entire week. IVs, oxygen masks, large doses of penicillin and myriad other drugs quashed the bacteriological assault. Worse, missing seven days of basic training usually leads to repeating the entire cycle, with rare exception. I was that rare exception.

The week I missed was heavy weapons training. My job, ostensibly, was to be able to close in and destroy the enemy in combat. For this you would assume I needed to know how standard Army weapons functioned. Sadly, my illness took me out of the field while my training company learned the art and functionality of the M-60/M-240B machine gun, the M-203 grenade launcher and the M-249 squad automatic weapon. I fully expected to recycle the entire course due to the fact that I had missed such an integral part of basic training. However, the leadership in my company decided to advance me towards graduation which—I thought at the time—was an incredible stroke of good luck. I had dodged a huge bullet!

But going through all of basic without firing three of the main four weapons left me with a grave deficiency. I began to feel deeply insecure about my lack of education commensurate to my fellow trainees, and to boot I had quickly discovered a distaste for life "in the field." This was obviously not the ideal recipe for a young man who had selected infantry combat arms for a profession. How I wished I had said yes to air traffic control and the six years associated with it.

Two choices remained: quit and pack my bags like 11 of the 44 men who began my training cycle or be the best soldier I could be and serve my country to the best of my ability despite my shortcomings. I chose the latter.

I may have been a mediocre field infantryman, but I did have qualities to offer the Army. I had dexterity, hand/eye coordination, better-than-average intelligence, deep patriotism, a complete lack of "stage fright," and strong communication skills. When I learned of the rare option to serve my country in the 3rd United States Infantry (the Old Guard) I couldn't sign up fast enough. This was my grand opportunity! I had found somewhere I could truly put my talents to work in an honorable fashion and erase the seeming deficiencies that plagued my conflicted mind. Come hell or high water, I was determined to succeed, just across the Potomac River and Washington itself in the U.S. Army's most celebrated, ceremonial unit. I finished basic, pinned on my paratrooper jump wings from subsequent training, got behind the wheel of my beat-to-hell '93 Ranger, and headed for our nation's capital.

F*cking College E-4s!

I called the duty station of my new unit the night before arrival, asking what uniform I should report in. The soldier who answered the phone told me, and I quote, "Dude, just wear civvies," meaning civilian clothes. Fantastic! I wouldn't have to cobble together a proper Class A uniform in a hotel room. What a break!

When I walked into the staff duty office late on a weekend in August 2000, I met two *highly pissed off* soldiers. Military life is hard enough and having to work a desk on a precious would-be day off enrages the average soldier. Your cohorts are off gallivanting around the playground that is the Military District of Washington and there you are, glued to a desk. It's like detention after school, but for 24 hours.

"Nice fucking uniform, new dick." This was my rageful greeting to America's regiment! After the requisite dressing down and after the Staff Sergeant determined I had been properly belittled, he escorted me to my new home for the next three years, Bravo Company. I was shown to my barracks room, a completely empty hallway, as the company was "in the field" at the time. I set my bags down on a mattress that looked like it came from the LBJ era military (it probably had) and took in the scene. A rat scurried across the air conditioning outlet into a vent. An ashtray piled with more butts than the Marlboro Man himself could muster. Ceiling tiles leaking. Furniture rusting. The central bathroom so disgustingly contaminated you would have to wear flip flops so as not turn your feet colors while showering. It was at that moment I decided a life selling computer equipment in corporate America actually did seem pretty damn fulfilling.

My squad leader was Staff Sergeant Aaron Barnes. Picture the fictional Staff Sergeant (SSG) Barnes from the film *Platoon* and substitute chewing tobacco for cigarettes, and you essentially had my squad leader. The Army utilizes a recruiting tool to lure in college grads in the enlisted sector; if you hold a bachelor's degree from an accredited institution, you immediately assume the rank of E-4 (E-1 being the lowest, E-9 the highest). It's an instant leap of three paygrades. SSG Barnes was not a fan of this particular policy, and he let me know it on a daily basis.

Barnes' right-hand man was a buck sergeant (SGT) named Tim Pennartz who held a similar view of the "college E-4" policy that, by the way, only the Army had at the time. Both of these men had earned each of their shoulder stripes the old-fashioned way, through active sacrifice. SGT Pennartz was as vocally "fond" of the "insta-rank" as his boss was.

Although I would not mimic their leadership style when I one day pinned on three chevrons, I owe these two men a debt of gratitude. I want to be blunt: I HATED them at the time. However, without Barnes and Pennartz, I would have likely floundered for three years as a tubby desk clerk, doomed to a life answering the company phone or mopping floors. They transformed a somewhat entitled and poorly conditioned E-4 into a real Old Guard soldier. As life would have it, 11 years later, Aaron Barnes even served as a groomsman in my wedding. The richness of God's irony could not be more profound.

SSG Barnes transformed me physically. He knew I was the worst soldier in the squad in terms of physical training. He would beat this out of me, nearly literally. Barnes also helped knock me down a rung or two on the entitlement ladder. I didn't realize it at the time, but in hindsight I recognize that I didn't know my place. Yes, I had private sector life experience. Yes, I had finished college. Yes, I might have had more book knowledge than my colleagues—but that didn't make me better than them. Certainly not in that environment. And I failed to realize that at the moment. My squad leader wouldn't tolerate that type of smugness. Though his methods were harsh, Barnes transformed me from a flabby, Scottsdale college boy into a soldier worthy of service in the Old Guard. I melted fat, built muscle, and learned to hold my own. More importantly, I began to treasure my fellow soldiers for their real value. His dedication to physical fitness and discipline stuck with me. For about a decade after the sun set on my military career, I still worked out at a gym five days a week and swore off fast foods. I owe that to Aaron Barnes, who would leave the service in early 2001. He is a dear friend to this day.

SGT Pennartz transformed me ceremonially. Not a big proponent of "positive reinforcement," his instruction was equally stiff, and failure was met with the stick—he didn't ever hold a carrot. Pennartz had a fantastic eye for detail and ceremonial accuracy. When SSG Barnes departed we had a replacement squad leader, but it was Pennartz who carried the baton of Patriarch of the Squad. In the end, he called the shots. This man taught me how to properly carry a casket, learn all six positions of the casket bearer team, and fold a United States flag into a crisp precision. Conducting a military funeral was not a job with our squad, it was an art. We were an *exceptional* team. We rehearsed our funerals the way the Radio City Music Hall Rockettes practice for the Thanksgiving Day Parade. Training was constant, repetitive, and it required a perfect outcome. Pennartz would lead us to back-to-back regimental awards for top six-man funeral squad. I never met a finer ceremonial soldier than Tim Pennartz. When he transferred to a unit in Korea, I would pick up the mantle of casket team leader and guide our team to a third consecutive regimental award. Aaron Barnes and Tim Pennartz taught me what I needed to know, and I will always be grateful for the knowledge and transformation they helped achieve in me. I would need every bit of it when a 24-year-old Bob Williams found himself a crow's flight from the Pentagon on September 11, 2001.

America on Fire

Memory is a fickle thing. The older you get, typically the less concise a mind's recollective capacity is. In my case I find it to be even more challenging. When I attempt to reconcile the precise sequence of events of 9/11, I feel I have it right. But as I said, the mind can be fickle. Think of it like this; when you brew coffee, the water is strained through the grounds using a filter barrier. The idea is that the delicious nectar you find in your cup is pure liquid, void of impurities. In this metaphor, I think of my recall as a mental coffee brewing. Memories are extracted from the reaches of the brain and strained through a filter of accuracy. As with even the most delicious cup of coffee, you still find some grainy dregs at the bottom of your cup. The grains are elements of inaccuracy. Alas, memory is an imprecise process unless you are a walking Smartphone. In the subsequent description of events, I will attempt to give you pure coffee. If a few grinds find their way into the cup, it was certainly not my intention.

After 18 months in service, I passed the Non-Commissioned Officer Promotion Board and was slated for promotion to sergeant in a month or two. I wasn't a sergeant yet, but rather a Specialist E-4P. The "P" stood for promotable. With that first advancement comes additional responsibilities. Namely, being on the mildly unpleasant rotation for junior level supervisory duties such as the Charge of Quarters (CQ), a function very similar to the military version of detention, though it is administratively necessary rather than being a punitive measure.

In late August 2001, the World Bank was headed to Washington, D.C., for a conference regarding the International Monetary Fund (IMF). The IMF was a controversial group. Their mission is to play a central role in the management of worldwide financial shortages and crises. They lend money to countries in need, but usually this comes with a foothold of the lender into the country of the lendee on an investment basis. However, there were political factions here and abroad that held a great distaste for the World Bank/IMF. Said protesters were usually young, unemployed and spoiling for a fight. They believed the IMF was economically invading and exploiting poor, needy countries. Opinions will vary on this topic, but what was certain was that a demonstration was sure to take place in early to mid–September when the IMF convened for their conference. Often, those demonstrations got out of hand.

The Washington, D.C., police were obviously the first line of defense in the event of a violent protest. If they found themselves outnumbered and overwhelmed, our unit was one of the available backup options. The Old Guard would periodically train for this situation. On the morning of September 11, 2001, I believe we had just completed riot training in lieu of our standard physical training session. Batons beating against plastic shields, advancing side-by-side with your fellow soldier-turned-law enforcement agent, chanting "get back" to your would-be attackers … all pretty basic stuff. At training's conclusion, we headed back to our barracks to shower, change and get into Battle Dress Uniform (BDUs).

My job the rest of that day was to be on the CQ desk. I returned to the barracks, showered and changed, ate a quick meal and threw an unhealthsome amount of tobacco dip in my cheek, before moseying downstairs to assume my post. Meanwhile, Bravo Company went about its business during what was scheduled to be a detail week.

(Quick Note: The cycle of functions for a line unit at the Old Guard was divided into three weeks. Primary Week: Funerals all day in Arlington National Cemetery, usually five or six. Backup Week: Filling funerals the primary company could not handle. Detail Week: Field training, DC or post parades, public ceremonies, wreath laying at the Tomb of the Unknown Soldier, etc. Basically, detail week was anything not related to funerals.)

I had banked on a rare lazy day, manning the CQ desk into the wee hours of the morning, listening to my subordinate "runner" talk about the merits of Video Game A vs. Video Game B while I shined my boots and attempted to stay awake.

Shortly after situating myself behind the desk in the lobby, the news broke. America would never be the same, and the world erupted into a state of conflict that has now lasted 18 years. The television screen on our old big screen projected the horrendous image of a plane hitting the first World Trade Center tower.

It was surreal. Soldiers never stop talking, never stop insulting each other, never stop bragging, almost constants in the day-to-day functionality of an infantry line unit. But in this moment, around 0840hrs, everyone fell silent. It was only after a sustained, dread-filled pause that a nearby NCO deadpanned, "These guys fucked with the wrong country." Very succinct words, and not much else needed to be said.

The attack on America that we would later learn came from rabid, foreign ideologues would quickly hit much closer to home … and in short order.

At approximately 9:45 a.m. EDT on 9/11/01, the unmistakable and repetitive noise of police and fire sirens penetrated the walls of our barracks. We threw open the doors leading outside and saw a parade of emergency vehicles heading at high speeds for Highway 110, which backed up against our post and cemetery. We wondered where they were headed.

An order was issued to assemble in our company quad area where we would receive important information and duty instructions. Normally when you receive typical briefings at the company level, it comes from a high-ranking NCO delivering the information. More specifically, the Company First Sergeant (1SG; highest enlisted rank for this size element) is the orator of news and instruction, if the information involved is routine. We only dealt with officers if we were getting an award or a figurative ass-whipping.

When our commanding officer "Captain A" took charge of the company, he delivered a somber announcement. Not only had multiple planes hit the World Trade Center, but one had also just hit the Pentagon—right in our backyard. American Airlines Flight 77 had slammed into the hive of American Military Intelligence and Planning, the Pentagon! Who attacks the Pentagon and the World Trade Center? Who? Only insane ideologues following a perverse guiding light, that's who. But we didn't know at the time who had authored this carnage. Captain A was blunt in the limited intelligence he had received and what awaited us. The building was on fire, people were dead, and the country would need the help of the Old Guard and more specifically, Bravo Company. Keep in mind, the Pentagon was a two-mile drive from where we stood in that Bravo Company quad, give or take. If you were a crow, you could have flown from our assembly point to the Pentagon itself in about a mile. So close you could almost touch it.

This was the extent of the information we had at that point. And what was a rare transparency of information flow, I believed our CO knew very little more than what he shared with us. The immediate order was to draw our issued weapons. And live ammunition. Not blanks, but the real deal; 5.56 NATO approved for use with an M-16 military carbine. My thoughts of course drifted to whether or not the IMF protesters were involved. Would we face armed conflict with live ammunition with our fellow countrymen? As much as I hated their politics, actions and beliefs, firing on your countrymen was a detestable prospect. This fear was quickly dispelled with the supplementary dispensation of data.

The Towers in New York, the fields in Pennsylvania and the Pentagon had all been hit by passenger liners. But by who? Why? It was a twisted mystery at that point, which only compounded our tension. Later we learned those flights were piloted by members of a radical terrorist (is there any other type of terrorist?) group of Islamic followers, the infamous Al-Qaeda.

Our destination the following morning would be the Pentagon itself. Bravo Company, 3rd U.S. Infantry would serve in a Rescue/Recovery effort in hopes of finding evidence, clearing the rubble, and the faint hope of finding survivors. One reads of nasty earthquakes around the globe where buildings are shaken to the ground, and two or three days later a paramedic or soldier finds a human being clinging to life, but alive nonetheless. This was my faint hope, and that of many other soldiers.

Fire Departments from D.C., Virginia, and Maryland were putting out the immediate flames and tending to the Pentagon personnel who were able to escape from the areas surrounding the impact area. At this point it was late in the day; darkness had already fallen. The final order was clear: No one would leave the company area, we would bed down in place where you could find space for a few hours' shut eye, and Bravo Company would head to the Pentagon first thing in the morning. We had work to do, and this great nation needed our help.

Inside the Pentagon

Early September 12, our company assembled with all the necessary gear for a week, plus material for our would-be home in the parking lots and grassy knolls that surrounded the Pentagon.

Bravo Company trucked out in vehicles known as "Deuce-and-a-Halfs." I assume the name came from the trucks ability to haul 2.5 tons of men and material, but even to this moment I have never thought to verify that. The front cab held driver and passenger. The back was a flat, metal bed surrounded by fencing, overlapped by green burlap-like material covering the truck. Picture the truck Indiana Jones assaulted from horseback in *Raiders of the Lost Ark*, and you have a very similar vehicle. When leaving Fort Myer, the rear flaps were withdrawn so we soldiers could see everything we left in our wake. Our convoy consisted of six to eight military vehicles and was led, and trailed, by military police cars.

Upon reaching the post's exit for Highway 110 leading to the Pentagon, the military police held traffic—and it wasn't light traffic. When our truck turned heading south, we saw a sea of civilian vehicles at a standstill behind the police cars. It was a most stirring sight, to say the least. Men and women, young and old, black, white and brown (and I would imagine liberal and conservative) were all standing outside their vehicles clapping, honking and waving small American flags. It was breathtaking. Inspiring. If only America

Firefighting men and machinery confront the damage (photograph by CPL Jason Ingersoll, USMC).

would not wait for a national tragedy to unite and put aside our petty differences, imagine what we could accomplish.

I think we all tried to play it cool at the moment so as not to seem overly emotional. To do so would be breaking ranks with the testosterone-times-10 level required at all times of each infantryman. But in that moment, my fellow soldiers realized for *the first time* the gravity and impact of the situation.

Arriving at the Pentagon yielded a sobering but expected situation. The building was not ablaze, but still smoldering. Fire crews were trying to put out flames at flare-up points and allow for safe access to the building. About 24 hours had elapsed since American Flight 77 hit the building. Heat emanated from the western wall. A makeshift crew of various local police, federal law, and military had begun to set up positions. In a space the size of two football fields, no more than a *literal* small stone's throw to impact point, the Old Guard had constructed a large tent alongside a small but extremely busy group of FBI personnel, Army Engineers and a smattering of police agencies. That day, I would venture no more than 700 people in total were at the site of one of the worst attacks to hit American soil since Pearl Harbor. I was one of them. It didn't hit me then, but I found myself at a cross-section of significant (and horribly tragic) history.

Senior leadership of not only our company, but also our regiment was briefed by the FBI, NTSB and the Corps of Engineers. As a lowly E-4, it's hard for me to say what transpired precisely in the tents of power 50 feet away. What I do know, however, is that we soldiers would be the instruments of those orders.

The Pentagon wall, one of the most heavily reinforced on the planet, looked to have a small opening leading to the interior impact point, about ten feet squared. It was there that all rescue and recovery personnel would first enter.

You hear about earthquake situations where two or three days later rescuers find someone clinging to life beneath boulders shifted aside by exhausted rescuers. This was our hope, and what was conveyed to us in the briefing by our Company First Sergeant and Captain.

"Look for survivors, look for evidence, and remove the debris by hand. If you hear the klaxon sounding, it means that the building might collapse. If you hear this get out in a military fashion."

That was it. That would be the mission for the next two weeks. We would enter the building about 36 hours after terrorists decided it would be a good idea to fly 64 innocent people into it at 500 mph.

Wearing only our BDUs, combat boots, Kevlar helmets, and surgical masks and gloves that resembled gardening mitts, we marched into the narrow opening for our first look inside the crumbling structure. It looked rickety. At best.

"Holy shit." I believe that was the unanimous statement by almost every soldier. The smell was what hit you first. We were not wearing any respirators or gas masks or other filtering devices. The smell. World War II veterans often talk about the stench of burning fuel and scorched metal and stinking wreckage that stayed with them forever, one of the most pungent memories of their later years. I was fortunate enough never to see the horrors of combat, but I did encounter that smell and I know of what they speak. To imagine the smell, think of your kitchen blowing up because of a gas leak, multiply that by ten, put out the flames and walk in. That would give you an idea of the aroma. I don't know why but the smell sticks with me to this day.

Huge chunks of concrete and metal rails, wiring, plaster, concrete and more concrete lay in front of us, a mammoth amount of debris. The Pentagon is made of five concentric rings. The impact of the aircraft and the accompanying blast had completely obliterated the outer, first ring at that southwestern section. It had badly damaged and shattered the second ring. Rings three and four had lesser damage but were affected, nonetheless. Only the fifth, innermost ring remain untouched.

There was no floor. Only somewhat navigable pieces of ground and rubble that were two to eight feet high, mixed with depressions of the surface. Tough to find a foothold to search and work.

Liquid was EVERYWHERE. A sharp, foul mixture of water, bodily fluid, jet fuel and whatever else the wreckage had spewed. We trudged through a sludge that easily reached the laces of your boots. Sometimes we'd sink to our ankles. Nasty stuff.

The Pentagon looked like the inside of a Halloween funhouse, the kind that simulates a decrepit, old mansion falling apart around you. But this was no fun house. The old mansion was indeed falling apart around you. Sirens would occasionally blare as we rushed out of the building, mortar and beams creaking and strange debris raining down. Often the sirens screamed and there was no falling from the sky, our Chicken Little moments, if you will. But the interruption to work was not seldom, and the trepidation, constant.

Except for beams of exceptionally powerful artificial light, the rooms were dark. It would be hard to find a foothold climbing on rubble or look for evidence unless it was a dayshift inside the badly damaged Pentagon. Bravo Company would not have dayshift duties. Bravo Company would only operate at night on 12-on/12-off shifts while a second Old Guard Company relieved us for the days while we slept and ate in the parking lot.

Bravo Company began an assembly line no different than you would find in a 1920s fire crew battling a blaze. Hip to hip, alternating positions on each side of the line facing each other. Concrete chunks, parts of a desk, wire, rebar, all passed down man to man for hours on end. We cleared a manageable path that first shift, making way for more efficient work on the second. If one questions why no backhoes or Bobcats were brought into action and why we relied on human power, the reason explained to me was to preserve the scene as best as possible. A crime scene should be disturbed in the most minimal manner in search of answers and evidence. Construction equipment wasn't an option. Grunts were.

No sign of life. No live bodies. I don't think any of us held out much hope after that first day. It was clear what we were looking at wasn't an earthquake. The fuel, the metal, the building … far too much to allow for a living creature's survival. We knew our mission moving forward would shift from rescue to solely recovery. We could find evidence. We could find the broken remains of our fellow citizens. That would be our collective goal.

At the beginning of day two, various Federal agencies arrived to support the operation. They alerted us that wearing only boots and BDUs into the war-zoned Pentagon was dangerous, not only because of the chemical and biological hazards created by the crash, but also because the World War II-era structure had been built with asbestos. Each soldier now entered wearing a sterile, white chemical and element-retardant suit (chemsuit), as well as a respiratory mask and surgical gloves. Upon exiting, we would get sprayed down with some water-based cleanser as a precautionary measure, before helping each other strip out of the protective outer layers.

Days two and three yielded evidence that made irrefutable the facts of an airplane attack. I find it tragically comic when I hear conspiracy theorists spout wild concepts that President Bush or the CIA attacked our own building with a missile—that there never really was a plane, that it was CGI-foisted on gullible Americans. What a farce. I was part of a two-squad level element that helped roll and push a portion of an aircraft engine out of the way to clear a space to allow further progress into the beast. I can't prove who flew that plane, but I assure you, a plane it was.

Work came to a halt when Army chaplains walked solemnly past Ring One to the rear portion of Ring Two/Three. Here a small portion of the fuselage was discovered, recognizably whole, with two or three late passengers inside. Helmets removed, soldiers watched quietly as the corpses were covered in blankets and tarps, their knees and legs still in the position of a human occupying an airplane seat. These innocent souls who died due to no fault of their own were found relatively intact, still clutching the armrests as when their plane penetrated the building.

Day four I was shifted off of rescue duty for a day and assigned a most odd security detail. My charge was to hold an M-16 (without bullets) inside one of the building's corridors and check the identities of workers who would be returning for the first time. A weird job, to be sure, given that police would have checked the workers upon entry, Pentagon guards screened them with airport-style metal detectors upon entering the building, and a security badge would have verified them entering the clearance areas of their assignment.

Nonetheless, my low level of authority wasn't meant for contemplation of rationale, but for execution of orders (and my life in the Army would have been much easier if I had grasped that concept sooner). Without ammo or any form of enforcement, a fellow soldier and I checked IDs and cleared that area for entry.

At the same time, my fellows of Bravo Company cleared the area sufficient for entry into the second level of the impact area. A squad of soldiers made its way upstairs looking for fresh areas of evidence. They found a most macabre scene.

Several officers and NCOs slumped over a conference table in a manner that almost resembled them having been anesthetized for surgery. They had not been burned or blown up, because American 77 had impacted the building in such an awful way that it was as if the plane were a knife cutting a piece of cake. Most of this section remained, as if it had just been sliced away from the other portions of the building. The areas closest to the "slicing" were still impacted, however. If one were to have been in these rooms, they likely would have died from the most severe concussion possible. The blast had created such a percussion wave that it ended the lives of the men and women nearby due to the impact of the brain against the skull. The passing of these souls would have been fast, nearly instantaneous. It was in this strangely preserved state that Bravo Company found these fallen comrades.

The days would go on … they would get easier. Eventually civilian support agencies rolled in and provided us hot meals, basic things like toothpaste and socks, and a taste of home. Outback Steakhouse, the Red Cross, and the Salvation Army all offered free meals, clothing and an outpost for a break. What a blessing these folks rendered.

Even in the most tragic and serious of moments, one must try to keep one's sanity and clarity using basic, lighthearted humor. Continued and insufferable grief leads to madness, or worse. As casket teams at the nation's most honored ground, we were constantly surrounded by sadness and misery. Now, more so. Thus, like undertakers and combat vets, we'd maintain at least some degree of laughter even in the most trying of circumstances. With this in mind, I decided to procure for our unit access to a vile vice that most soldiers find themselves adhering to—chewing tobacco.

Being short on time, and without access to shop for the good stuff, I had a bright idea. A fellow soldier and I made an inquiry to the largest dip company in America at the time, U.S. Smokeless Tobacco. We asked if they might rush a box of dip to the cargo area that served as the support area for supplies and material flowing in for the Pentagon recovery. We offered to pay.

The good people at U.S. Smokeless did us one better, freighting in a small pallet of every dip they manufactured. Skoal Mint, Copenhagen, Grizzly and more. They even included a greeting card signed by their Public Relations staff thanking us for our rescue efforts. I think perhaps Americans at this time just wanted in some way to do their part, whether it was donating blood or blankets, or in this case, bringing in 400 cans of fine tobacco.

Concealing a pallet full of vice brought with it some concern that the officer leadership might take exception to my procurement plan. Fears of being punished mounted; if the Captain took a dim view of the situation, it would not work out well for me. Upon receipt of the goods, the Captain inquired, "Williams, did you really get a pallet of free chewing tobacco brought out here?" I answered in the affirmative and held my breath. You can imagine my relief when he simply responded, "Can I get a can?" I couldn't press a log of fresh Copenhagen into his hands quickly enough.

Hijinks aside, we had more work to do. Shifts inside the Pentagon continued, 12 hours on, 12 hours off. More rubble removed, more evidence recovered. The rubble morphed from large boulder-sized elements of conglomerated concrete and rebar, requiring chain-gang style exertion from dozens of men, to simple blocks of debris we could hand carry. Remnants trickled down from pieces of plane fuselage to a burnt third of a person's pocket wallet.

After the better part of 10 days, the path to the building's downstairs emerged. When the FBI deemed the site to be nearly clear of any other valuable evidence, our efforts stopped being rescue/recovery and just became cleanup. The worst kind of cleanup, I suppose. Heavy equipment became the tool of choices, and the forklifts and backhoes rolled in.

On the eve of the penultimate day of Bravo Company's Pentagon mission, I was informed that I had passed the promotion board to sergeant. My platoon sergeant told me I needed to take a physical fitness test the following day. Unfortunately for Bob "Squirrel" Williams, while this PT test was being conducted, President Bush and Secretary of Defense Rumsfeld visited the disaster site to thank the Old Guard and all responders for persevering at a difficult time and a difficult place. I missed this memorable moment, which ended that part of Operation Noble Eagle, the name assigned to the operation we had conducted.

Our work was done. Now began the task of fighting a war against those that brought this suffering to our doorstep.

I would not take up arms against those who launched the attack on our great nation. However, probably 60 percent of the men I served with at the Pentagon would go on to this fight that never ended and may never end. Some of them would not make it back and our country would never be the same. I would never be the same. Not a day goes by when I don't think about my time at the Pentagon after September 11. I didn't realize it at the time, but I do now; I had found myself at a cross-section of history, albeit horrible history. Instead of being a part of the 99 percent of Americans who watched this terror unfold on TV and opened up their wallets to donate to the Salvation Army or donated blood at the Red Cross, my fellow soldiers and I were fortunate enough to physically do something that day. Bravo Company would not be firing bullets back at the bad guys during those two weeks in September of 2001, but by busting our asses among the wreckage and fumes and fluids in that collapsing building, I like to think we provided some hope. Maybe the soldiers of Bravo Company, the Old Guard, launched the first salvo back against those that hated us, even if it was only a salvo that testified to the unbroken spirit of this great nation.

I never served in combat. "You go where the Army tells you," as the saying goes, so I spent the majority of my remaining service burying the fallen in Arlington National Cemetery. Only now it wouldn't be 85-year-old World War II veterans who had passed from natural causes; the deceased would now often be 19 or 25 years old. Our mission became very different, and we conducted that mission with vigor and determination.

On December 26, 2002, I was honored to address our company in a brief farewell before the soldiers and officers of Bravo Company before they filed out for Christmas. Afterwards I packed in an empty locker room area and empty barracks. It was eerie being in that place all alone with just my thoughts. Before I walked out, bags slung over my shoulder, wearing my uniform for the last time, I thought of what took place at the Pentagon and what we did. I thanked God I was able to serve my country at that time, at that place. I was gratified beyond recognition that I could do my part, even if only a small one. I closed the door behind me and left the service a grateful man.

Back to Barbecues, Ball Games and Babies

Seven months after my discharge, I ended up back where I began, in Phoenix. For good and for bad, it's home. I transitioned from Army green uniforms to corporate black suits and began a career with FedEx as an Account Executive that goes on even now. It's a quality organization, and I earn a quality living.

Between 2003 and 2011 I had more than my fair share of fantastic life experiences. I swam with sharks in the Caribbean, hoisted lagers in Bavaria, drove race cars, took private pilot lessons, and packed more adventures into eight years of single life than I can effectively enumerate. I lived "the good life." But a funny thing happened, I eventually fell in love. Hey, it happens to the best of bachelors!

When I met Emily, she struck me as a kindred soul, despite our decade age gap. We found immediate commonality in religion, politics, travel, and good southern barbecue. Most importantly, we quickly determined that—more than anything else—each of us wanted a family. We craved the white picket fence, the two cars and the 2.2 kids. I married above my paygrade with that woman, a world-class wife and now mother.

My five-year-old son, Teddy, is the apple of my eye and a source of great pride. Every day, he astounds me with his passion for learning and his kind heart. Ava, my three-year-old daughter, is the jewel of my heart and object of great devotion. She's a firecracker, and already strong and independent. She's also a daddy's girl and has me wrapped around her little finger.

My wife and children are the greatest gifts I ever received from God Almighty. I got more than I deserve. My family is everything to me ... *everything*. When I lay eyes on Emily, Teddy and Ava, I am reminded of all that's right with the world. They are all that is good and wholesome, and nothing that is devious or unkind.

Dreams often take me back to Ft. Myer. Images of the relationships I built, the service we rendered to our country, the camaraderie, and yes, the Pentagon are indelible in my mind. People often say that when you die, your life flashes before your eyes. If that's true, when God calls me my final thoughts will undoubtedly and deservedly be of my family, but I sure wouldn't mind if He gave me a preliminary detour. I would treasure a momentary visit to one of those moments wearing Old Guard Blue and Army Green. Those are cherished, special moments beyond description. It's funny how you never know you are having the time of your life until it's all over.

For the Old Guard Soldiers Unspoken and Unsung

Mark Joseph Mongilutz

A handful of special souls have given of themselves herein. They have formed with their collective memories an accounting of truth and of pain, of childhood memories and of adulthood traumas, of lives compelled to serve and of hearts forever reshaped by the toll exacted thereby.

But these special souls represent scarcely a sliver of those TOG soldiers who took part in the Pentagon Recovery Effort, to say nothing for Operation Noble Eagle in its vast and enduring entirety.

This closing chapter is an echo of the words, the memories, the reflections, and the wounds of those who, like each of this work's contributors, took part in the 9/11 Pentagon Recovery Effort while serving with the 3rd United States Infantry Regiment (the Old Guard), but whose voices might otherwise exist only in obscurity. I cannot speak for them in any direct capacity and would feel disinclined to do so if asked.

But I can say things *of* them. And will.

They set themselves to work of a violently morbid and endlessly grueling sort, a sort so very far removed from that normally expected of them. They steeled themselves for sights they could, only days earlier, never have fathomed encountering, certainly not on United States soil. They looked to one another for support ... and received it. They looked within themselves for strength ... and found it. They searched for purpose through it all ... and realized it had always been there; but the sacrifice that thrust it into proper relief was always too great. Too many lives lost, families shattered, dreams corrupted. It was too much. If that is the price of purpose, we might consider renegotiating with the powers that be.

Still, I am not personally acquainted with a single TOG brother who would not once more affix the respirator to his face and enter the site of

A flag whose presence meant so much (photograph by Jocelyn Augustino).

impact in hopes of transforming an episode of despicable evil into a single moment of painfully extracted goodness. And I trust this is the case for all those to whom this essay is dedicated.

And there were indeed so many. Hundreds upon hundreds of regimental soldiers doing what was asked of them. Some struggled with the psychological shock, others with the physiological stress. But such struggle was shared by all. We did not know how to fight back nor if our combined strength would ever be brought to bear against those responsible, but we knew there was work to be done where we stood. That had to be enough for us in that moment, and we had to be enough for one another throughout the innumerable moments that would follow.

Those moments continue to accumulate, strengthening the bonds between us still further.

To those many TOG soldiers who labored throughout the Pentagon Recovery Effort but are unspoken in this book, we do hear you. We know what you endured, and we are one with you in bearing its persistent burden. Our lives have diverged over the ensuing years, but our shared sense of purpose, a purpose born of tragedy, has linked us one to the next in perpetuity.

We hear you.

Farewell: An Epilogue

Mark Joseph Mongilutz

As far as any mortal creature can assert with certainty, we will make our way through this lived experience a total of once. We've one chance to do good, or not. One chance to be worthy, or not. One chance to create an unwritten record of actions, some commendable, some regrettable, most neither.

One chance for all of it. One fleeting breath in which to say something meaningful, or to simply exhale as an ephemeral expression of our having once been.

One chance.

I'll speak for my brothers only in attesting the following thoughts: Whatever it is any of us did prior to our part in the Pentagon Recovery Effort, and whatever it is we've done since, those days of wading through the physical and emotional wreckage of so hideous an atrocity certainly registered as a sea change for us all, one whose brutality saw fit to scar us, one whose exigencies inevitably bonded us, one whose implications persistently stalk us, and one whose sacrifices created in us a sense of shared understanding whose temporal resilience might well carry forth until the last of us has perished.

The recollections whose words you have absorbed herein carry with them information, certainly, a shared chronicling of the days following September 11, 2001, as experienced by soldiers of the Old Guard. But those words also impart lessons and meaning which jointly venture beyond the borders of imperfect testimony and into the realm of larger meaning.

Mining the caverns of memory in search of painful truth, of something useful to the human experience, of perspective that might otherwise wither into oblivion—in that process there is meaning. Not one among the contributors whose experiences are printed on these pages successfully transcribed their recollections without confronting long-dormant demons. Forgotten horrors, suppressed emotions, merciless regrets, guilt. To one degree or another, those phenomena comprised the itinerary for every soldier or veteran who elected to give of themselves in contributing to this work. That much is deserving of acknowledgment, perhaps more so than whatever appreciation one might feel in sorting through timeline specifics and related minutiae.

Lastly, since engaging with the first of the essays to reach me, I have come to truly recognize the fragility and vulnerability of memory for what it is. Soldiers with whom I stood and labored throughout this period remember things differently than do I. They remember things differently than one another. We reflexively prioritize elements of the Recovery Effort in ways our peers and others present might not; we are left with distinctive retellings of a story which nevertheless ring true as a whole. Confronting that phenomenon alone is enough to justify the undertaking of this effort.

And now, having organized, edited, and reflected upon these materials as I have done, saying anything more would amount to an exercise in editorial indulgence, and so I'll say nothing more for the time being. Other than to bid you farewell, that is.

Farewell.

Glossary of Commonly Used Terms and Acronyms

ANC   Arlington National Cemetery.
APFT   Army Physical Fitness Test.
ASVAB   Armed Services Vocational Aptitude Battery.
Battlehard   Moniker of The Old Guard's Bravo Company; also "B Co." (see "Company" below)
BDUs   Battle Dress Uniform.
Company   Soldier grouping consisting of approximately 100 to 120 soldiers; an organizational sub-structure with which soldiers tend to strongly identify. (See "Battlehard")
11Bravo (11B)   The MOS (see below) designator for a U.S. Army infantry soldier.
Fort Benning   An Army post located in Georgia; recognized and referred to as "The Home of the Infantry."
Fort Myer   The since-renamed post on which most of The Old Guard operates (Alpha Company operates out of Fort McNair because ... well, they seem to prefer it that way).
Kevlar   A proper noun, as many are surprised to learn. Not unlike the classic example of "Kleenex."
MDW   Military District of Washington.
MOS   Military Occupation Specialty; the code denoting one's profession within the military. (See "11B")
NCO   Non-Commissioned Officer; a term applicable to ranks falling between E-5/Sergeant and E-9/Sergeant Major.
"New Dick"   Soldier who has recently reported to their military unit/duty station.
PT   Physical Training.
PTs   Uniform worn while engaged in Physical Training.
Recent Richard   See "New Dick."

ROP Regimental Orientation Program; training regimen unique to The Old Guard during which newly arrived soldiers are drilled in standing manual, ceremonial marching, et cetera. Pronounced "rope" because the alternative sounds odd.

TOG "The Old Guard"; historical moniker of the 3rd United States Infantry Regiment (coined by General Winfield Scott).

About the Contributors

Adam **Behrens** is a mechanical/civil engineer and lives in Littleton, Colorado. After military service he obtained a degree in engineering from George Mason University. He first went to work as a construction engineering inspector for the Army Corps of Engineers and then worked for the Federal Highway Administration as a project engineer. He currently works as a patent examiner in the field of intellectual property for the United States Patent and Trademark office. He is married and the father of two.

Christopher M. **Bradley** served in the United States Army from 1998 to 2002, and was honorably discharged at the rank of Sergeant E-5 after serving in the 3rd United States Infantry. He resides in North Carolina with his wife Tammy and their five children. He currently works with children in care of the Department of Social Services.

Dennis **Brady** (known mostly as just Brady) grew up in the woods of the Matanuska-Susitna Valley of Alaska. A career soldier, he lives with his wife Margaret, their daughter, his mother-in-law, and their old dog about an hour north of D.C. Although he is currently stationed in South Korea as a physician assistant, he is looking forward to retiring from the Army and continuing to practice medicine closer to home.

Larry **Carter** II is from Lansing, Michigan. He attended Michigan State University, from which he earned a degree in electrical engineering. After college, he became a process electrical engineer for 3M before enlisting in the United States Army in September of 2000. He joined the Old Guard, serving in Bravo Company before then becoming a bomb technician and an officer in the U.S. Army. He is married and has three children.

Marshall R. **Codd** retired from the U.S. Army in 2018 as a Chief Warrant Officer Three (CW3). He and his family moved back to the Upper Peninsula of Michigan, near the city of Marquette, where he works seasonally with the U.S. Forest Service. During his off season he is a stay-at-home father and plays in a local band.

Eric **Ebner** is from Lafayette, Louisiana. He spent a lot of time in his youth at Pecan Island, where he worked cows, fished, and got into general mischief with his two

About the Contributors

brothers and sister. He is the proud uncle of four nieces and a nephew, and lives in Houston with his girlfriend and their dog.

Matt **Genkinger** is from Iowa. He served in the U.S. Army from 1999 to 2011 first as an infantryman assigned to the 3rd U.S. Infantry Regiment (The Old Guard) and later as a Human Intelligence Collector, embarking on several overseas deployments. He currently works and resides near George Washington's Mount Vernon. His boys, Frank and Hayden, will come to know him much better when they read his recollection of September 11, 2001.

Andy **Graff** is a middle school language arts and creative writing teacher residing among the high desert mountains of Utah. He worked for two years as a senior writer for RSL Soapbox on SBNation. Among the publications in which his work has appeared are *Exoplanet Magazine* and the *Chronos* anthology. He is a graduate of Western New England's MFA program.

Jonathan **Hoffman** was born in Dayton, Ohio, in 1978, to Simon and Irmgard Hoffman, of Beavercreek. He currently lives in western Germany while finishing his Army career. He has a daughter, Julia, and two sons, Benjamin and Finn. He hopes to retire from the Army very soon and continue in government service.

Fines E. ("Eddie") **Kiper** II lives in San Antonio, Texas, and works as a criminal investigator/digital forensic examiner. He is married with two children and enjoys woodworking and a wide variety of outdoor activities in his spare time.

Mark Joseph **Mongilutz** is a professional ghostwriter, copywriter, and author. He lives in Scottsdale, Arizona.

William Arthur **Roum** is currently both an employee with the United State Department of Veterans Affairs and a small business owner. He lives in Castle Rock, Colorado, with his family, Amber, Payton, Odin, and Jax. In his current position, he has extended his personal commitment to aid his fellow veteran and fellow man, while gaining acceptance into the University of Colorado, Skaggs School of Pharmacy.

Brett (Thurman) **SanPietro** served in the Old Guard as an enlisted infantryman, 2000–2004. Subsequently, he received commissions as an Intelligence Officer in both the Army and the Navy, served eight years as a career diplomat with the U.S. Department of State, and is now the Midwest Regional Director for Team Red, White, and Blue, a veteran's service organization. Originally from the Detroit area, He and his wife Lara now reside in Chicago with their dog, Riley.

Robert Earl **Williams** separated from the Army as a proud member of The Old Guard in December of 2002. He latched on shortly thereafter with FedEx Services as an account executive, negotiating contracts with potential customers. He thrives in that profession today. Bob married Emily Gorbutt of Goodyear, Arizona, in 2011, and they have two children, Theodore Lee and Ava Rae, his true passion and love in life.

Index

AAR (after-action report) 14
Afghanistan 37, 65, 67, 74, 85, 95-96, 107, 114-115
Air Assault School 18
Air Force ROTC 87
Airborne School 9, 50, 61-62, 99, 108, 121
al Qaeda 135
Alcohol, Tobacco, and Firearms (ATF) 45
Alpha Company 32
American Airlines Flight 77 10, 36, 104-105, 112, 119, 134, 136, 139
Amtrak 66
anthrax 95
A.P. Hill, Fort 67, 81
Arlington, TX 103
Arlington, VA 13, 69-70, 88, 103, 122
Arlington Ladies 114
Arlington National Cemetery (ANC) 4, 9, 12, 21, 36, 44, 50, 61, 64, 67-70, 73, 74, 80, 88, 95, 100-101, 103, 107, 114, 118, 133, 141, 149
Army Corps of Engineers 16, 151
Army Physical Fitness Test (APFT) 8, 149
ASVAB 17, 26, 60, 76, 128, 149
Audie Murphy 128

barracks 26, 28, 35, 41, 50, 52, 56, 61, 63, 69, 71-73, 75, 78, 81, 90-91, 100, 102-104, 110, 112-113, 119-120, 124, 129-130, 133-134, 141
Basic Training 9, 18, 27, 40, 76, 88, 100, 110, 129; Infantry Basic Training 99
Battlehard (Bravo Company) 18, 19, 21, 24, 51, 56, 70, 89, 149
Beltway 96
Belvoir, Fort 77-78, 89, 95
Benning, Fort 9, 18, 46, 49, 60, 67, 97, 99, 108, 121-122, 128, 149
bin Laden, Osama 28
Birdwell, Brian 38
black box 13
Blackhawk Down 70
Bobcat 36, 138

body bags 20
Boeing 757 92, 94
Bragg, Fort 99, 108, 114, 133
Burger King 40, 106, 124
Bush, George W. 17, 76, 101, 108, 139, 141

Caisson Platoon (TOG) 9
Capitol 19; Capitol Building 78
Capitol Police 19
Casket (Platoon/team) 50, 51, 64, 89, 100-101, 140
caskets 18, 23, 52, 89, 93, 100-101, 131, 132; casket bearer 118, 131
Cessna 68, 90, 102
charge of quarters (CQ) 68, 80, 81, 111, 133
CIA 95, 139
Clinton, Bill 3, 37, 76, 101
CNN 28, 117
COIN 96-97
Colors Squad 96
Columbarium 53
Columbia Pike 70
Crystal City 12

D.C. Sniper 114
DEA 22-23, 63
Decision Points 107-108
Delayed Entry Program (DEP) 49, 99
Department of Defense (DoD) 92
Desert Storm 28, 67
deuce-and-a-half 43, 91, 104, 135
DiLorenzo Clinic 29, 31-32
Djibouti 37, 95-96
Domenici, Pete (senator) 100
Dover (Air Base Force Base) 74
drill sergeant 18, 26, 40, 110
Drill Team (U.S. Army) 9

Echo Company 41, 76, 80-81
Edsall Road 104
82nd Airborne 98-99, 114
11Bravo (11B) 50, 72, 99, 149

154 Index

Emergency Response Team (Pentagon) 30
Engineers (Pentagon) 34, 36, 56, 62-63, 92, 95, 123
Expert Infantryman Badge (EIB) 52, 81-82

F-16 103
FBI 13, 14, 31, 36, 41, 44, 92-95, 107, 136-137, 141
fighter (jet) 11, 31, 71, 103
firefighter 31, 34, 62, 71, 73, 92, 95, 123
Flight 175 90
Fort Myer 9, 19, 34-35, 50-51, 53, 57, 60-61, 64, 67, 70-73, 77, 78, 80, 88-89, 100, 105, 110-111, 113, 122, 135, 142, 149
Fort Myer fire department 80
Full Honors 64, 70, 89, 101, 107

George Mason University 74
George Washington University 100
Georgetown 29, 111
GI Bill 8

hazardous material (hazmat) suits 13, 84
Headquarters and Headquarters Company (TOG) 76
Henley, William Ernest 39
HMMWV 50, 69-71
Home Depot 32, 34, 64
Horn of Africa 37, 64, 74

International Monetary Fund 88, 132-134
Interstate 66 (I-66) 69, 71
Invictus 39, 40-41, 46
Iraq 37
Islamic 21, 70, 135
Isuzu (moving truck) 23
IV 30-31, 38, 129
Iwo Jima Memorial 91

Joint Readiness Training Center (JRTC) 67

K9 22, 24
Kevlar (helmet) 32, 69, 72, 92, 111-112, 123, 137, 148
Key Bridge 29
Knox, Fort 98
Korea 24, 38, 118, 132, 151; Korean War 67, 101
Kosovo 127
Kremlin 96

Lemonnier, Camp 37
LMTV 73, 91, 112

M Street 29
M16/M16A2 68-70, 85
M40 field protective mask 68
M939 (personnel truck) 12
Malvo, Boyd Lee 113

Manassas 114
Marine Corps (U.S.) 8, 18, 25-26, 104, 109, 123, 128
Maude, Timothy (lieutenant general) 95
McDonald's 21
medic (Pentagon) 31
Military District of Washington (MDW) 28, 61, 88, 130, 149
Military Police 17, 43, 69-70, 111, 113, 135
Mueller, Robert 95
Muhammad, John Allen 113

National Capital Region (NCR) 41, 113
National Guard 29, 67, 81, 114, 125
National Mall 9
Navy (U.S.) 8, 35, 44, 60, 78, 98-99, 125, 128 152; Navy Reserves 125
New York City (NYC, New York) 1, 10, 25, 29, 45, 62, 68, 102, 119, 123, 134
NOK 52-54
North Parking Lot (Pentagon) 29, 31, 33, 36
Nuclear, Biological, Chemical (NBC) 68

Obama, Barack 96
Old Post Chapel 70
Operation Noble Eagle 23, 32, 37, 95, 107, 141, 144
Outback Steakhouse 21, 81, 106, 140

Panama 28, 72
Patton Circle 74
Pearl Harbor 102
Pentagon City 23
Pentagon: damage 1, 4, 12, 15, 19, 20, 32, 44, 56, 70, 73-74, 79, 104, 112, 122-123, 136-139; evacuation 29-31; fires 34, 56, 62, 105, 122; point of impact 10, 36, 68, 70-71, 91, 104, 119, 122, 134; impact witness 12; rings of 13, 31 137, 139
plane parts 12-14, 20, 22, 33, 74, 95, 112-113, 139
Polk, Fort 19
post-traumatic stress 16
Potomac River 88, 92, 100, 111, 130
Powell, Colin 44
Puerto Rican National Guard 92

Red Cross 21, 94, 106, 140, 141
Regimental Orientation Program (ROP) 9, 28, 50, 100, 150
Remembrance Ceremony (9/11) 14
Ronald Reagan Washington National Airport (Reagan National Airport) 9, 111
Rosslyn 71
ROTC (Army) 97-99, 127
Route 27 91
Rumsfeld, Donald 95, 106, 141
Russell Senate Office Building 100
Russia (Russian) 23, 36, 96

S-3 (Operations) 76-77, 81
Section 60 (ANC) 70
Section 64 (ANC) 91
Section 68 (ANC) 36
Soldier's Medal 37
Sorensen, Kris 29-32, 37
Sousa, John Phillips 127
South Washington Blvd 36
Southern Baptist Men 21
Spann, Johnny "Mike" 95
Spirit of America (SOA) 61, 90
Starbucks 124
Summerall Field 80
Swindell, Charles 115

Taco Bell 81
Taliban 97, 115
30th AG Battalion 49, 60, 76, 99
Tenza Terrace 19
Tomb of the Unknown Soldier 9, 101, 133
triage station (Pentagon) 30-31
Twilight Tattoo 67

Twin Towers 10, 55
Tyvek suits 32, 34, 63, 112-113, 123, 124

U.S. Highway 50 69, 72
Unity, Camp 94
USO 94

Virginia State Police 69

Washington, D.C. 9, 11, 19, 27-29, 45-46, 51, 62, 64, 68, 74, 81, 87, 100, 107, 111, 115, 117, 132-133, 135, 151
West Point 97, 126, 128
White House 18, 68, 76, 78
World Bank 88, 117, 132-133
World Trade Center 1, 18, 28, 41, 68, 77, 90, 102, 111, 117, 134; South Tower (South WTC Tower) 62, 90; Twin Towers 10, 55; The Tower/towers 28, 44, 103, 133-134

Yooper 50

www.ingramcontent.com/pod-product-compliance
Ingram Content Group UK Ltd.
Pitfield, Milton Keynes, MK11 3LW, UK
UKHW042016140426
5217IPUK00015B/1214